Twelve Step Sponsorship
HOW IT WORKS

Twelve Step Sponsorship

HOW IT WORKS

Hamilton B.

HAZELDEN®

INFORMATION & EDUCATIONAL SERVICES

Hazelden
Center City, Minnesota 55012-0176
1-800-328-9000 (Toll Free U.S., Canada, and the Virgin Islands)
1-651-213-4000 (Outside the U.S. and Canada)
1-651-213-4590 (24-hour FAX)
http://www.hazelden.org (World Wide Web site on Internet)

Library of Congress Cataloging-in-Publication Data
B., Hamilton.
  Twelve step sponsorship : how it works / Hamilton B.
    p.   cm.
  Includes bibliographical references (p.   ) and index.
  ISBN 1-56838-122-0
  1. Alcoholics—Rehabilitation—United States. 2. Twelve-
step programs—United States. I. Title.
HV5279.B18   1996
616.86'106—dc20   96-28947
                                                        CIP

04 03 02 01   10 9 8 7

Book design by Will H. Powers
Typesetting by Universal Press & Link
Cover design by David Spohn

Editor's note

The Twelve Steps and Twelve Traditions are reprinted and adapted
with permission of Alcoholics Anonymous World Services, Inc. Permission
to reprint and adapt this material does not mean that AA has reviewed
or approved the contents of this publication, nor that AA agrees with the
views expressed herein. AA is a program of recovery from alcoholism
only—use of the Twelve Steps in connection with programs and activities
which are patterned after AA, but which address other problems, or
in any other non-AA context, does not imply otherwise.

*To Father Tom Butler, who is not an alcoholic or addict,
but who has led many people to Twelve Step recovery.
My close friend and spiritual advisor, he inspired me
to write this book. I am deeply grateful.*

Contents

Preface

This book is about sponsorship in Twelve Step programs and the significant difference it can make in recovery. The principles and guidelines it describes are based on the model of sponsorship developed by Alcoholics Anonymous. Most of the examples in this book are taken from AA literature, the original source on Twelve Step recovery. My own experience has been in AA. It is in AA that I first found a sponsor and learned how to be a sponsor.

But you don't have to be an AA member to use this book and to make it work for you. *Whatever Twelve Step program you call home, you'll find that the principles and guidelines—and the experience, strength, and hope—will fit.*

**AA created the concept of sponsorship,
but its principles apply to all Twelve Step programs.**

In some Twelve Step Fellowships, the Twelve Steps are almost exactly the same as those in AA. In others, the Steps have been altered slightly more to reflect the particular addiction, compulsion, or focus of the group. In Narcotics Anonymous, for example, the phrase "our addiction" has been substituted for "alcohol" in the First Step and "addicts" for "alcoholics" in the Twelfth Step. In Overeaters Anonymous, the word "food" has been substituted for "alcohol" in the First Step and "compulsive eaters" for "alcoholics" in the Twelfth Step. Despite the slightly different wording, however, the fundamental principles of recovery remain the same in all the Twelve Step programs.

It was not practical to write a book for *each* of the different Twelve Step Fellowships (which now number over sixty), nor was it necessary. In those instances where the fit among Fellowships is not exact, I have used AA as the model with the expectation that the reader will make whatever wording adjustment is necessary to make the principle apply to his or her Twelve Step program. For example, direct quotations from AA literature use the terms "sober," "alcohol," "alcoholism," and "sobriety." In some instances, I could not alter the original AA text to make it more inclusive without distorting its meaning.

In general, I have used the word "recovery" rather than more specific words such as "sobriety," "abstinence," or "clean" since it is an awkward use of language to use "clean, sober, abstinent" every time the reference is to not drinking, not using, or not engaging in compulsive behavior. Likewise, I sometimes use the word "addict" to refer to someone who suffers from any kind of addiction or compulsive behavior. Occasionally I use the term "sobriety" to stand for all forms of abstinence since that term is used in many programs besides AA.

The individual literature of each Fellowship also presented a referential problem. The basic textbook of Alcoholics Anonymous is entitled *Alcoholics Anonymous* and is affectionately referred to as "the Big Book." Other Fellowships also have basic texts (for example, *Narcotics Anonymous* and *Overeaters Anonymous*) which also have their own nicknames ("the Basic Text" in NA, for example). I have chosen to use the phrase "basic text" or "Big Book or equivalent" to refer to the basic textbook of a Twelve Step Fellowship. Likewise, I have used AA's term "Conference-approved" to mean literature approved by any Twelve Step Fellowship as representing its official position. While non-Conference-approved literature can often be very helpful, it represents the opinion of its author and not the Fellowship.

> *Most Twelve Step programs have a basic textbook*
> *which is the equivalent of AA's "Big Book."*

For those readers who are not AA members, the numerous references to AA's Twelve Promises may be unclear. The Promises are a group of benefits that AA members receive after having painstakingly worked the first nine Steps of the AA program. The Promises include "a new freedom," "a new happiness," "serenity," and "peace." It is my belief that these same Promises are fulfilled in the lives of other Twelve Step Fellowship members who painstakingly work the Steps. The Promises are listed in appendix B (page 228).

A word about personal pronoun usage in this book: When I am referring specifically to my own AA sponsees, I use the masculine pronoun because my AA sponsees are all male in accordance with AA tradition. When I am making a reference to sponsees in general, on the other hand, I use both the masculine and feminine pronouns or a pronoun that is gender neutral. Some historical quotations use only the masculine form when referring to both men and women, in accordance with the traditions of the time.

None of these changes to make the book more inclusive is important, however, and none dilutes its basic purpose. What *is* important is that each of the Twelve Step programs offers a way out of our addiction, compulsion, or problem *if we are willing to work the Steps.* In all the programs, the Steps are the key to a rich and fulfilling recovery. An important part of working the Steps in every Twelve Step program is having a sponsor. Being that sponsor or finding that sponsor is what this book is about.

Sponsorship is one of the greatest adventures and greatest rewards of Twelve Step recovery. Through it, you can create one of the most meaningful and enduring relationships of your life. That, at least, has been my experience with sponsorship, and it has been the experience of countless others. It can be your experience as well.

Sponsorship is part of the promise
that we "never have to be alone again."

Acknowledgments

I want to thank my sponsor, David S., for his wisdom and support over the years and for his detailed and perceptive review of the manuscript which made a significant difference in the book. David introduced me to the term "grandsponsor," meaning, "your sponsor's sponsor," a term I have used because it captures the love that is part of sponsorship. "Grandsponsor" reminds us of the collected wisdom in Twelve Step groups that is handed down from one generation to the next within this family of our choosing.

I also want to thank Ed S., Fionnula F., Rod C., and Jeanne R. for their insights on sponsorship which I have incorporated into the book. My special thanks to Dennis W. for all his help and suggestions. I want to express my gratitude to Harold H., a remarkable man who has helped me and many others in so many ways, and to Ken B. who got me to my first AA meeting.

Most important, I want to thank my brother Herbert for his faith in me and for his love and support during the "best of times and the worst of times" as I struggled to learn and apply the principles of the Twelve Steps in my own life. His patience and steadfastness have been remarkable.

I am grateful to AA World Services for their continued efforts on behalf of all of us in the Fellowship and for their generous permission to quote so extensively from AA sources. They are a dedicated group of individuals carrying on the loving tradition established by Bill Wilson, Dr. Bob, and the other AA pioneers.

And, of course, my profound thanks to my sponsees past and present for all they have taught me, but especially: Andy B., Brian B., Byron B., Chris D., John K., David L., Dick M., Henry S., Dave T., and Warren T.

I want to thank some special members of the Fellowship whose words and lives have meant so much to me in my sobriety: Anne B., Allan C., Ed C., Mike D., Abigail G., Lauder G., Mark G., Tim G., the late Tom G. (who gave me my first Big Book), Ann H., Harry L., Candy M., Hal "Attitude of Gratitude" M., Gay Q., Dede S., Sandy S., the late Sandy S., Marijane V., and Steve W. Without these wonderful AA members and hundreds of others who share their experience, strength, and hope with me, I could not have stayed sober.

My God bless you and keep you on the Road of Happy Destiny.

Introduction

When I was new to Alcoholics Anonymous, people in the Fellowship suggested that I find a sponsor. But how was I to find one? And where? And, most important, who would it be? The AA Big Book didn't mention sponsorship, and there were no books written about it. I was scared to ask someone to sponsor me, so I put off getting one. I kept thinking I could do it myself. I couldn't. Now I see how much not having a sponsor delayed my progress in AA.

**When I was new to AA and looking for a sponsor,
I didn't even know the right questions to ask.**

After a while, I did get a sponsor. Then one day, someone asked me to sponsor him. Suddenly, I had a big responsibility. I had dozens of questions that I wanted answered. And quickly. What was I supposed to do as a sponsor? How would I know when he was ready to take a Step? What if he drank? I had nothing to rely on but my own sponsor and what I had heard about sponsorship in AA meetings and from other sponsees.

Twelve Step Sponsorship: How It Works came out of those early sponsorship experiences and out of the fear and earnestness I saw in my own sponsees when they were asked to sponsor somebody for the first time. They had many questions, but AA's only publication on this topic was a thirty-page pamphlet called "Questions and Answers on Sponsorship." So when a friend of mine made the suggestion, I decided to write something that would guide Twelve Step members through the sponsorship process.

The result is a guide for both sponsors and sponsees, for both newcomers and old-timers. *Its purpose is to help sponsors be the most effective sponsors they can be, and to help sponsees get the most they can out of having a sponsor.* Because my experience and knowledge are mostly in AA, the ideas here will reflect mainly an AA perspective. Yet, this book will be useful to people in any Twelve Step Fellowship — e.g., Al-Anon, Narcotics Anonymous (NA), Cocaine Anonymous (CA), Overeaters Anonymous (OA), or Adult Children of Alcoholics (ACA) — who want to take advantage of the special resource of sponsorship.

This book discusses what a sponsor does, how to find a sponsor, and how to be a sponsor. It also explains how to help a sponsee work each of the Twelve Steps.

This book is a guide to the sponsorship process.

The suggestions in *Twelve Step Sponsorship* did not originate with me. Everything in the book comes from AA through its members, meetings, and publications, but it is filtered through my perception. The only real authorities in AA are the Big Book (entitled *Alcoholics Anonymous*), *Twelve Steps and Twelve Traditions*, other Conference-approved literature, and decisions of the AA General Service Conference (as AA's elected voice). These sources are largely silent on sponsorship, so most of what is in this book comes from my own experience and from the experience of other AA members. As with AA, the only authorities in other Twelve Step Fellowships are their Conference-approved literature and their equivalent to the General Service Conference.

In the process of writing *Twelve Step Sponsorship*, I have discovered just how different opinions are within the Fellowships regarding sponsorship. Part of the reason is that there is no authoritative book on the subject that we can all use as a common reference point. Instead, we have relied on what our own sponsors have told us and on what we have heard in meetings. Sponsorship has been a word-of-mouth phenomenon. The result is that the contents of this book do not necessarily represent a consensus of opinion within AA on sponsorship. The book represents my considered opinion and the opinions of those with whom I have spoken while writing it. *Twelve Step Sponsorship* is not an AA, Al-Anon, NA, OA, or CA Conference-approved book. In the best Twelve Step tradition, use what you can and leave the rest.

In the best Twelve Step tradition, use what you can.

Many AA and other Twelve Step Fellowship members will not agree with the detailed suggestions and commentaries in this book, although I believe they will largely agree with its four major points. Those points are as follows:

1. The primary responsibility of sponsors is to help their sponsees work the Twelve Steps.
2. A sponsor and sponsee have an obligation to discuss their mutual expectations, objectives, and requirements, if any, regarding the sponsorship relationship *before* they enter into that relationship.
3. A sponsor shares his or her experience, strength, and hope with his or her sponsee rather than trying to run the sponsee's life.
4. A sponsor must never take advantage of a sponsee in any way.

Sponsorship is intensely, wonderfully personal. Each of us brings our own ideas, strengths, and weaknesses to it as both sponsors and sponsees. No one is an "ideal" sponsor and no one is a "perfect" sponsee. Thank God. But we can all learn to be better sponsors and better sponsees. Undoubtedly, there are certain native talents to the sponsorship art, but there are also some principles that can be brought to bear. Those with a load of "talent" still need to understand the guidelines. Those with less natural "talent" can improve their effectiveness by increasing their knowledge about sponsorship. No set of rigid rules could possibly do the phenomenon of sponsorship justice, but it is my hope that the observations in this book can begin to capture its spirit.

As with all teacher/student relationships,
it is difficult to tell who learns more:
the sponsor or the sponsee.

The Easy Way to Use This Book

Twelve Step Sponsorship: How It Works is not a book that has to be read from the front to the back.

Start reading wherever you want.

The book is divided into three parts and twenty-one chapters to make it easier for you to find the subjects that most interest you. The table of contents lists the specific topics covered in the book. There you can find the subject you want to read about first and get started right away.

**Check the table of contents
for a list of topics covered in the book.**

Part I, "Finding a Sponsor," is primarily aimed at sponsees, although it was also written for sponsors. It describes what a sponsor does, offers suggestions on how to choose a sponsor, and answers some questions that sponsees often ask.

Part II, "Being a Sponsor," is primarily aimed at sponsors, although it was also written for sponsees. It describes the responsibilities of sponsors, discusses sponsor/sponsee expectations, offers suggestions on how to introduce a newcomer sponsee to a Twelve Step Fellowship, and answers some questions that sponsors often ask.

Parts I and II of the book
contain frequently asked questions
about sponsorship, sponsors, and sponsees.

Part III offers a step-by-step framework for a sponsor to guide a sponsee through each of the Twelve Steps. This section gives a brief history of the Twelve Steps and provides sponsors with ideas for helping sponsees study and understand them.

Part III contains a Step-by-Step guide
for helping a sponsor work each of the Twelve Steps.

The appendices is a reference section that contains the AA Preamble, AA's Twelve Promises, the Twelve Steps of various programs, and the Twelve Traditions.

There is also an index at the end of the book that contains an alphabetical list of the major subjects discussed and their page numbers. The index makes it easy to find a given topic quickly.

Check the index for page
numbers of specific topics.

The purpose of this book is to teach you about Twelve Step sponsorship and, therefore, to help you be a more effective sponsor and a more knowledgeable sponsee. Read the book all the way through, or skip around to the parts you need. Use the book in the way that's most effective for you.

PART I

Finding a Sponsor

1

What Does a Sponsor Do?

In some ways, a sponsor is like a good friend, a wise teacher, a private tutor, a favorite uncle, a seasoned mentor, an experienced guide, and that older brother or sister we always wanted but never had. Sponsorship, which includes aspects of all these roles, is nevertheless unique. A sponsor is someone who has been where we want to go in our Twelve Step program and knows something about how we can get there. His or her primary responsibility is to help us work the Twelve Steps by applying their principles to our lives. Sponsorship is a basic part of belonging to a Twelve Step Fellowship and potentially one of its richest experiences. Sponsorship can be, like friendship, one of life's great blessings.

**A sponsor's primary responsibility
is to help a sponsee work the Twelve Steps.**

But sponsorship can also be a scary experience, at least at first. We become vulnerable whether we want to or not. We take on responsibilities and develop expectations. We take risks. We reveal who we are and unload our secrets. We let another person into our lives in an honest and intimate way. We drop our facade. It can be frightening as well as exhilarating to trust another human being and to build a relationship with him or her.

This chapter describes some of the reasons for overcoming a

natural reluctance we have to share our lives and our secrets with another human being. It explains what a sponsor does and, therefore, why it's important to have one. But first . . .

A Brief History of Sponsorship

The idea of sponsorship was born in Alcoholics Anonymous, the original Twelve Step Fellowship. *Living Sober,* an AA publication, describes how the term "sponsor" came about.

> In the earliest days of A.A., the term "sponsor" was not in the A.A. jargon. Then a few hospitals in Akron, Ohio, and New York began to accept alcoholics (under that diagnosis) as patients—*if* a sober A.A. member would agree to "sponsor" the sick man or woman. The sponsor took the patient to the hospital, visited him or her regularly, was present when the patient was discharged, and took the patient home and then to an A.A. meeting. At the meeting, the sponsor introduced the newcomer to other happily nondrinking alcoholics. All through the early months of recovery, the sponsor stood by, ready to answer questions or to listen whenever needed. Sponsorship turned out to be such a good way to help people get established in A.A. that it has become a custom followed throughout the A.A. world, even when hospitalization is not necessary.[1]

Sponsorship has since become one of the foundations of the recovery programs of all Twelve Step Fellowships and one of the greatest blessings of membership.

What a Sponsor Does

AA defines sponsorship in this way: "An alcoholic who has made some progress in the recovery program shares that experience on a continuous, individual basis with another alcoholic who is attempting to attain or maintain sobriety through A.A."[2] Every sponsor is different, just as each sponsee is different, but certain activities, responsibilities, and obligations are common in sponsor/sponsee relationships. The primary ways in which a sponsor shares his or her experience, strength, and hope to help a sponsee are as follows.

A sponsor helps us work the Twelve Steps
by providing explanation, guidance, and encouragement.

Helping a sponsee work the Steps is a sponsor's most important function. The Twelve Steps are the foundation of AA and other Twelve Step recovery programs. The Steps require us to take action, but they were not meant to be worked alone. In fact, we cannot work them alone if we follow the way the AA Big Book suggests that we work them. The meaning of the Steps and how they are applied to life require explanation and interaction. A sponsor can help us translate the general principles of the Steps (a set of ideas) into the specific activities of our lives (our behavior).

A sponsor can provide some temporary discipline and motivation as well as the ongoing encouragement that we may need to work the Steps. There are times that call for "tough love" in sponsorship. Our sponsors can help us resist looking for an easier, softer way than working the Twelve Steps and applying their principles in our lives. They can confront us on our procrastination and on our unwillingness, when necessary, and help us stay focused on what's improtant—Fellowship principles and the work of the Steps.

A sponsor helps us get established quickly in our Fellowship
by explaining basic concepts and terminology
and by introducing us to other members.

A Twelve Step group's unfamiliar language, customs, and ideas can be confusing to newcomers ("turn it over," "ninety in ninety," "easy does it," and "keep it simple," for example). A sponsor can guide us through this confusion by explaining the Fellowship's customs, concepts, and terms. By teaching us the language of recovery, our sponsor can help us understand the program more quickly and help us feel part of it sooner.

A sponsor is a safe person whom we can learn to trust.

Most of us have a lot of fear, many questions, and more than a few secrets when we come into recovery. In order to get better, we need to share our fears and our secrets with someone else and find the answers to our questions. Our sponsor is the person in our Fellowship who feels the safest and is best suited to help us do that. Sponsorship creates a safe environment in which we can expose a little bit of who we are. Addiction is a disease of isolation and loneliness. Having one person whom we can trust and with whom we can share our feelings and fears helps reduce our loneliness and isolation. A sponsor provides a safe place for us to be honest about ourselves and to discover the rewards of being open with another person. As the AA Twelve and Twelve says, ". . . We don't have to be alone anymore."[3]

**A sponsor can answer the many questions that we have
as newcomers or develop as "mid-timers."**

As newcomers to a Twelve Step program, we can ask our sponsor "dumb" questions, "ridiculous" questions, terrifying questions. Our sponsors can provide one-on-one answers to satisfy our curiosity, increase our understanding, and reduce our fears. They can do the same even after we've been in recovery a long time, because as we grow in recovery, our questions don't end. We have new experiences, face new challenges, and develop greater insights that lead us again to our sponsors for their experience, strength, and hope. Our sponsors are deep reservoirs of practiced Twelve Step knowledge.

**A sponsor can help us in the process
of self-examination that the Steps require.**

Self-examination is a difficult process without the assistance and encouragement of another person. Self examination is a crucial part of any Twelve Step program. The Fourth, Fifth, and Ninth

Steps require it specifically (see the Steps beginning on page 229). Self-examination in the First Step requires us to look honestly at our powerlessness over our addictive substance or behavior and at the unmanageability of our lives. Later, we will have to examine our character defects and the harm they have caused. A sponsor can keep us honest in our program by pointing out when we are deluding ourselves about our addiction or our recovery. Being honest with our sponsor also increases our humility and helps us learn to live in reality rather than fantasy. A sponsor can help us through this painful, but necessary and rewarding, process of self-examination.

> **A sponsor encourages us to read the basis text
> of our Fellowship and other program literature
> and to engage in Fellowship activities and service work.**

As important as meetings are, a Twelve Step program is more than just meetings. Working the program also means using the Twelve Steps, reading the Big Book or its equivalent, changing our attitudes and behavior, doing service work, and carrying the message of recovery to other alcoholics or addicts inside and outside the Fellowship. A sponsor can encourage us to do all these things and remind us to use the various tools of our recovery program.

> **A sponsor can monitor our progress,
> confront us when it is appropriate,
> and generally help us stay on the recovery path.**

Our sponsor is in a unique position to keep track of our progress in recovery. He or she can often detect the warning signs of a slip even before we can. When we are on a "dry drunk" or are actively moving away from the program, a sponsor's intervention can often bring us back.

Most of us need to be confronted now and then on the kind of negative behavior that brought us to recovery in the first place.

How else are we going to change? But with our sponsor, the confrontation is not an attack. A sponsor confronts our *behavior*, not our being, and he or she does it with compassion. Sponsors can point out our inappropriate behavior and how it hurts us without making the confrontation a hostile act. They can do it because of their love and acceptance of us, and because of our willingness to trust them.

Sponsors can confront us on inappropriate behavior
as no one else can.

A sponsor reminds us to apply Twelve Step principles in our lives.

The Twelve Steps offer a "design for living" that means much more than not having a drink or not using (although *not having a drink or not using* is the basis of everything else that our Twelve Step program gives us). Our new way of life in recovery requires us to change some of our old attitudes, perceptions, beliefs, and behavior by applying these Steps and program principles to our lives. Because we are trying to learn to use new tools for living, we need someone to remind us to use those tools and to help us figure out *how* to use them. A sponsor can do that because he or she knows both us and the tools well.

A sponsor models the Twelve Step program of recovery.

There is a Twelve Step saying that "we have to walk the talk" to stay sober. It is not enough to theorize about recovery; we have to live it. Understanding what a Step means is only half of it. The other half is applying it. A good sponsor sets an example for us by showing us how to use Twelve Step principles to build a rewarding, sober life. By modeling the principles of the program, a sponsor becomes a powerful teacher. With such a sponsor, we can learn by doing as well as by example.

Our sponsor is available in times of crisis.

Especially as newcomers to recovery, we face fears, crises, and new circumstances that challenge us. We may suddenly want to drink or use. Or we want to know how to handle an unexpected situation. We may just need to talk. With a sponsor, we have someone we can turn to. We have someone who knows and cares about us who is available in times of crisis. (Even without a sponsor or when our sponsor cannot be reached, we can always turn to someone else in the program.)

*It feels good to know
that we can always call our sponsor.*

A sponsor provides practice in building relationships.

Our relationship with our sponsor can serve as a model for other relationships. We can practice expressing our feelings, revealing our fears, and discussing our expectations with another person. We can also practice admitting when we are wrong, making amends, and being honest. We can learn to trust and to ask for help and to think about someone other than ourselves. What we learn with our sponsor, we can then apply to other people in our lives.

In essence, with our sponsors and others in the program we can learn to experience and express love and to feel loved in return. Finally, we will come to love ourselves.

*A sponsor can help us achieve a
richer, deeper, more enjoyable recovery than
we are likely to find on our own.*

What a Sponsor Does Not Do

What a sponsor *does not do* is as important as what he or she *does* do. The following list describes some things a sponsor either cannot or should not do.

A sponsor cannot keep us in recovery.

Whether or not to drink or use or to engage in compulsive behavior is a decision we alone can make. No one else can make it for us. No one else can keep us sober. Not a family member, not a friend, not a boss, *and not a sponsor*. It is said in AA that sponsors "don't take the credit when their sponsees stay sober and they don't take the blame when they drink." The decision to stay in recovery is ours alone. We make it one day at a time with the help of the program and our Higher Power. Our Twelve Step Fellowship gives us the power of choice.

A sponsor is not our therapist.

Sponsors are not psychiatrists, psychologists, or therapists (unless they happen to be psychiatrists, psychologists, or therapists, but even then, they don't act in that capacity with their sponsees). It isn't a sponsor's function to provide therapy to a sponsee. There is no "treatment plan" other than working the Twelve Steps. All sponsors can do is share their experience, strength, and hope concerning their own recovery. They are not our therapists, and we are not their patients.

The Twelve Steps are about spiritual growth, not therapy.

A sponsor should not attempt to control our lives or encourage an unhealthy dependence.

No Twelve Step Fellowship ever tells a member what he or she *has* to do. The only requirement for membership is a desire to stop drinking, using, or engaging in compulsive behavior. Even AA's original Twelve Steps are merely "suggested." Whether or not to work the Steps is left entirely up to us. In the same way, it is not up to our sponsor to control our lives. Advice is a tricky thing because we never really have enough data about someone else to make a decision for him or her. Nor is it our responsibility to do so even if we could. Twelve Step programs emphasize sharing experience, strength, and hope with one another—not offering advice.

In a sponsee's early days of recovery, a sponsor may wish to make strong suggestions to his or her sponsee about what to do and what not to do. For example: don't drink or use, go to meetings, read the Big Book or equivalent, call your sponsor, and so on. But these suggestions are still suggestions. We are better off when our sponsor leaves the actual decision to us while describing the program principles and experience that are relevant to that decision. As sponsees, each of us should retain the responsibility for making the basic decisions about our lives, including the decision to stay in recovery.

A sponsor should not permit, much less encourage, a sponsee's unhealthy dependence. A sponsee's only dependence should be on the Fellowship and, ultimately, on a Higher Power. A healthy *interdependence*, however, always exists between a sponsor and his or her sponsee.

*Our only real dependence
should be on our Fellowship and a Higher Power.*

A sponsor should not take advantage of us or exploit us in any way.

The most fundamental responsibility a sponsor has toward a sponsee is *never to exploit* him or her in any way. In practical terms, it means that sponsors should not try to use their sponsees as a way to borrow money, make money, have sex, advance their careers, or do anything else that harms their sponsees or puts them at risk. A sponsor has a sacred trust toward his or her sponsee.

The relationship between a sponsor and a sponsee is inherently unequal because the sponsee is seeking guidance and has placed himself or herself in a vulnerable position. Even when there is no difference in the length of sobriety, a sponsor has a psychological advantage. In technical terms, a power differential exists that leaves sponsees vulnerable to manipulation. Morally and ethically, a sponsor may not take advantage of that vulnerability in any way whatsoever.

There are stories of sponsors who have attempted to abuse their sponsees for their personal gain. If a sponsor *ever* tries to abuse the sponsorship relationship by trying to do any of these things or anything like them, the sponsee should find another sponsor immediately.

> *A sponsor should never take advantage of us in any way.*
> *If he or she tries, find another sponsor immediately.*

2

Choosing
a Sponsor

Choosing a sponsor is something like choosing a friend. Sometimes it just happens and sometimes it's planned, but there is always something about the other person that attracts us. Picking a sponsor can seem like a long, difficult process. The purpose of this chapter is to make that process easier by providing some general guidelines. As there are exceptions to every rule, there are exceptions to these guidelines. But for the most part, they hold true.

This is a "how-to-do-it" chapter divided into four parts. Each part discusses a stage of choosing a sponsor:

CHAPTER CONTENTS

1. *Finding a temporary sponsor*
2. *Guidelines for choosing a primary sponsor*
3. *Interviewing a potential sponsor*
4. *If a potential sponsor says no*

Finding a Temporary Sponsor

Some Twelve Step groups have lists of members who have volunteered to act as temporary or "interim" sponsors for newcomers to the Fellowship or to the area. "Interim" means temporary. A temporary sponsor can ease our transition in a number of ways. He or she can answer our questions, explain program concepts and terms, introduce us to people, get us started on the Steps, and help us apply the new principles we are learning. Temporary sponsors are like primary sponsors except that we usually haven't spent a long time choosing them. Some temporary sponsors become primary sponsors, but many are replaced by someone else.

A temporary sponsor can help us with our recovery program while we look for a primary sponsor.

SUGGESTION: To find a temporary sponsor, ask the secretary or chairperson of every meeting you attend if the group maintains a list of temporary sponsors. If they have such a list, call some of the people on it. If you like what you hear on the phone, set up a meeting to discuss sponsorship. If there is no group list, announce in the meeting that you are looking for a temporary sponsor and ask for volunteers. Either way, you will more than likely meet members who can sponsor you temporarily while you look for a primary sponsor. Even with a temporary sponsor, be sure this person has some quality recovery behind him or her and is able and willing to give you the support you need.

Guidelines for Choosing a Primary Sponsor

Addiction is a dangerous, often deadly, disease. Most of us came to recovery because we were in desperate emotional trouble and had run out of other options. Now, what stands between us and active addiction is a program of recovery, including a support system for working that program. Staying abstinent is serious business despite the fun we often have. An important part of maintaining our recovery is finding a sponsor to help us work the Steps. The choice of a primary sponsor should not be haphazard or casual. It is not an exaggeration to say that we are talking about our *lives* here. What we want is a *real* sponsor who will make a significant contribution to our recovery and to our lives.

The best way for us to find a primary sponsor is to go to many meetings and look hard for one. By listening to enough people talk, we will find someone with whom we identify and feel comfortable. Usually, our sponsor turns out to be someone whom we respect and want to be like, and who has the kind of recovery program we admire.

> SUGGESTION: When someone at a meeting has things to say that you like, spend some time after the meeting talking with that person. Ask what meetings he or she regularly attends. Suggest that you have coffee before or after a meeting and ask for his or her telephone number. Make plans to meet so that you can learn more about each other.

> SUGGESTION: Ask your program friends who sponsors them. Remember that finding a primary sponsor is a process that can take some time.

A few guidelines will help in picking a sponsor you can work with effectively. As usual, there will be exceptions, but these are proven principles that have worked over the years.

SOME FACTORS TO CONSIDER IN CHOOSING A SPONSOR

1. *Has what we want*
2. *Lives in the solution*
3. *Walks the talk*
4. *Has a sponsor*
5. *Emphasizes the Steps*
6. *Has more time in recovery than we do*
7. *Has worked more Steps than we have*
8. *Is available for telephone calls and meetings*
9. *Emphasizes the spiritual aspect of the program*
10. *Gender is the same as ours*

Has what we want

Choose a sponsor who has the kind of recovery you want to have. Since a sponsor is someone who has walked the path you're about to walk, it makes sense to choose someone who has ended up, or at least seems to be heading toward, where you want to be. All a sponsor really has to offer is his or her experience, strength, and hope. So we want to be sure that our potential sponsor's experience, strength, and hope are the kind we want and need. The only way we can find out is to listen to what our potential sponsor has to say and observe how he or she behaves.

Choose a sponsor whose
recovery and life you admire.

SUGGESTION: In meetings, listen for people who say things that you relate to and that you find insightful and helpful. If you look forward to hearing someone speak, that person may be a good candidate for your sponsor.

Lives in the solution

All sobriety is not created equal, and length of sobriety is no guarantee of its quality. In choosing a sponsor, pick someone who lives in the solution and not in the problem. In other words, choose someone who seems to be working a solid recovery program. Listen to what your potential sponsor says in meetings. Find someone who talks about how he or she applies the Steps each day, who handles life competently and with expectation, and who has a positive outlook on life. Since a sponsor can only offer us what he or she already has, the last thing we need is old addictive thinking to guide us (even if the addict is clean, sober, or abstinent).

Walks the talk

Our potential sponsor's behavior ought to reflect the principles that he or she proclaims in meetings. Some people talk a good line in meetings, but they have not yet managed to translate that talk into behavior. There is a problem with being sponsored by such people. Since they have not been able to apply Twelve Step principles to their own lives, they will have difficulty helping us apply them to ours. Their unwillingness to look at their own character defects, for example, creates a blind spot that makes it hard for them to acknowledge our character defects and help us face them. We may learn recovery talk from such people, but we may not learn recovery behavior. And a Twelve Step program is a program of action.

Choose a sponsor who applies
Twelve Step principles to his or her own life.

Has a sponsor

In choosing a sponsor, pick one who has his or her own sponsor. Your sponsor's sponsor is sometimes called your "grandsponsor." Your grandsponsor is a resource for your sponsor when he or she has a question about your program. Your grandsponsor also helps your own sponsor stay on the recovery track. An AA member, for example, without a sponsor is not working the Steps in the manner prescribed by the Big Book, which means that he or she is unlikely to be able to help you work them effectively.

Emphasizes the Steps

Not all sponsors emphasize working the Twelve Steps to the same degree. Some will work closely with sponsees on the Steps and others will not.

SUGGESTION: Since the Steps are so important, choose a sponsor who will emphasize the Steps and work closely with you. Ideally, a sponsor will ask you to read the Big Book or equivalent and the Twelve and Twelve or equivalent, give you study assignments on the Steps, monitor your progress, and encourage you to move through the Steps as quickly as you can while still being thorough.

Choose a sponsor who will
work closely with you on the Steps.

Has more time in recovery than we do

As a general rule, a sponsor should have more time in recovery than we do (up to a point, of course), with one year of continuous recovery as a minimum. In theory, the longer the recovery time, the more experience, strength, and hope a sponsor will have to share concerning recovery. Furthermore, he or she will have been where we are trying to go. Therefore, everything else being equal, a greater period of recovery is preferable.

The one-year minimum guideline is as much for our potential sponsor's protection as it is for ours. Most Twelve Step members need that first year to get their own recovery in order before they are qualified to take on the considerable responsibilities of sponsorship.

Choose a sponsor with at least one year
of continuous recovery.

Has worked more Steps than we have

Our sponsor must have worked the Steps that he or she is going to help us work. AA is grounded in experience, not theory. If our sponsor hasn't worked a Step, he or she can't lead us through it. So we should choose a sponsor who has worked more Steps than we have (or the same number, if we have both worked all twelve).

Not every program member would agree, but I believe that potential sponsees should find a sponsor who has worked *at least* the first five Steps. That number allows a sponsee room to grow and ensures that his or her sponsor has completed the difficult Fourth Step and has examined his or her character defects with another person. If we get ahead of our sponsor in working the Steps, we need to find another sponsor.

Twelve Step groups are grounded in experience, not theory.

Is available for telephone calls and meetings

Not all sponsors are equally available for sponsee telephone calls and meetings. Travel schedules, work schedules, family responsibilities, social engagements, and personal preferences influence how often contact can occur between sponsors and their sponsees. Sponsorship works best when our sponsor's frequency of availability meets our need for frequency of contact. For that reason, availability is a factor in choosing a sponsor. The only way to determine whether or not the match will be a good one is to discuss it.

Discuss with your potential sponsor
how often he or she will be available to you.

Emphasizes spiritual aspect of the program

Since the Twelve Steps make up a spiritual program and since many people have difficulty with the spiritual aspect, it's important to know where our potential sponsor stands on this critical issue. Our sponsor can only share his or her experience, strength and hope with us. Therefore, only those who have a spiritual program can share it.

SUGGESTION: Ask a potential sponsor
· The degree to which he or she emphasizes the spiritual aspect of the program.
· Whether or not he or she is willing to work closely with you in developing your own spirituality.

Ask a potential sponsor how much he or she emphasizes the spiritual aspect of the program.

SUGGESTION: If you are not an atheist or agnostic, you probably should not choose an atheist or agnostic to sponsor you since you will have difficulty getting help from them with your spiritual program.

If you are an atheist or agnostic who is open to believing in a Power greater than yourself, choose a sponsor who will work with you on the spiritual aspect of the program. Otherwise, you will probably do better with an atheist or agnostic sponsor.

Gender is the same as ours

Same-sex sponsorships are preferable to opposite-sex sponsorships in the case of heterosexuals in order to avoid the possibility of a sexual relationship developing between sponsor and sponsee. Generally, a same-sex sponsor is also easier to identify with. In the case of gay men and lesbians, same-sex sponsorships carry the risk of sexual involvement. Therefore, certain precautions need to be taken which are the same as those for opposite-sex heterosexual sponsorships. (See chapter 5, "Sponsorship Expectations," for more information on the precautions.)

In a sponsorship where the risk of sexual involvement exists, certain precautions can be taken.

Interviewing a Potential Sponsor

We can theorize all we want about whether or not someone will be a good sponsor, but we won't really know until we do some investigative work. The only way to determine whether or not a potential sponsor will be a good match for us is to meet with him or her to discuss sponsorship. Such an interview with a potential sponsor can be an intimidating experience, especially when we're new to recovery. But the purpose of the interview is not judgmental. It is analytical. The question it seeks to answer is, "Do *we both* think sponsorship will work for us?" Sponsorship has to work *for both parties* or it won't work at all.

A program member who is a great sponsor for one person may not be as effective for somebody else. We don't all want the same style of sponsorship, but there is someone for each of us. By describing how he or she expects to conduct the learning experience called sponsorship, a potential sponsor can help us decide whether or not his or her course of study is what we had in mind.

In the interview, ask your potential sponsor whether or not he or she reads the Big Book or equivalent, makes study assignments, and will meet with you regularly. Ask what his or her expectations and requirements are and what he or she thinks the role of a sponsor is. Ask questions that are important to you, questions about the program, recovery, spirituality, the Big Book or equivalent, or personal data about your potential sponsor—whatever will help you determine if this person will be a good sponsor for you.

> SUGGESTION: Before meeting with your potential sponsor, review the guidelines for choosing a sponsor in the first part of this chapter. Also, check out chapter 5, "Sponsorship Expectations." Chapter 5 covers the basic issues you may want to discuss besides spirituality and working the Steps.

> *Both sponsor and sponsee should agree*
> *that the sponsorship match is right.*

Part of accepting responsibility for our sobriety is being thorough in choosing a sponsor. As newcomers, we can seek the advice and support of our temporary sponsor as well as trusted friends. We can even propose the topic of "finding a sponsor" in meetings. Finding a sponsor is a rite of passage in Twelve Step programs. It is a natural and important part of growing up in the Fellowship.

Remember that you don't have to do the interview perfectly, and if you make a mistake, you can always change sponsors.

Don't be shy about interviewing a potential
sponsor before deciding if the match is a good one.

If a Potential Sponsor Says No

We all fear rejection. It is a frightening prospect to think that we might finally get up enough courage to ask someone to sponsor us only to have that person say no. When we are new to recovery, we tend to think that such a rejection is all about us. It is usually not. There are many reasons why a potential sponsor might reject our request to be sponsored, none of which has anything to do with us. Some of these reasons are

1. The person is currently sponsoring as many people as he or she can handle. A sponsor who takes on too many sponsees does each of them (and himself or herself) a disservice.
2. The person is not taking on new sponsees because of a heavy travel schedule, a planned move, or some other reason based on where he or she is in life or the program.
3. After discussing the potential sponsorship, the person realizes that the match would not be a good one. That conclusion is as much about the potential sponsor as it is about us.

When potential sponsors reject our request
for sponsorship, it is usually about them.

Potential sponsors are usually careful to explain why they won't agree to sponsor somebody. After all, they were once looking for a sponsor themselves, and they remember what it was like. Also, sponsorship is a service opportunity that offers many rewards. Being a sponsor is one of the privileges of being a Twelve Step program member and one of the ways we stay in recovery. Therefore, the natural inclination is to accept a new sponsee.

When a member doesn't, it should be for a very good reason. Since members aren't perfect, however, it isn't always.

It's a privilege to sponsor someone.
And it's one of the ways we stay in recovery.

If a potential sponsor says no, it's important to move on and find somebody else to ask. While the rejection may be painful, at least we tried. And we learned something from the experience. The next time, we'll know more about the process. And we'll have something else to share with our own sponsees someday.

3

Some Questions Sponsees Ask about Sponsorship

This chapter contains a group of questions that sponsees and potential sponsees sometimes ask about Twelve Step sponsorship. The answers are based on my own experience and on consultations with other program members whose recovery I respect. Your own sponsor will be a valuable resource in helping you answer these questions. Not all program members will agree with the answers.

Who were Bill Wilson's and Dr. Bob's sponsors?

Bill Wilson and Dr. Bob were AA's cofounders. Ebby Thatcher was Bill Wilson's sponsor, and Bill Wilson was Dr. Bob's sponsor.

Bill and Ebby first met in 1911 when Bill was about fifteen. Ebby explained to a still-drinking Bill Wilson in 1934 how he had gotten sober in the Oxford Group. That meeting across the kitchen table in Bill's home ultimately led Bill to the Oxford Group and then to sobriety.[1]

> *Ebby Thatcher, who led Bill Wilson to sobriety in the Oxford Group, became Bill's sponsor.*

Father Ed Dowling was Bill's spiritual sponsor, and it was with Father Ed that Bill took the Fifth Step.[2] Dr. Sam Shoemaker, an Episcopal priest, also served as a spiritual advisor to Bill.

Is it okay to change sponsors?

Yes, it is. You can change sponsors whenever you want. However, it might be wise to consider your reasons for wanting to change. An examination of your motives is a precaution against any change meant to avoid facing something you don't want to face. One way to check your motives is to inventory them. Take a sheet of paper and list your reasons for wanting to change sponsors on one side of the page. List your reasons for *not* changing sponsors on the other side. Weigh the reasons for and against and ask your Higher Power to help you decide. Sleep on it. Then follow your intuition. You will intuitively know how to handle the situation.

We are free to change sponsors whenever we want.

Give serious thought to *not* changing sponsors if you are leaving your sponsor because he or she is pressing you on an issue that you don't want to face, or because your sponsor "knows you too well."

How is a spiritual advisor different from a sponsor?

Some Twelve Step members choose a nonaddicted spiritual advisor who they think is especially qualified to help them with the spiritual aspect of their program. They work closely with him or her just as they would with their primary sponsor, but their focus is on spiritual development. In essence, these spiritual advisors function as "spiritual sponsors" even though they are not members of a Fellowship.

Because Twelve Step programs are fundamentally spiritual, it is impossible to separate the spiritual from the work we do with our primary sponsor (unless we are atheists or agnostics closed to the idea of developing spiritually). For that reason, many members never choose a spiritual sponsor, relying on their primary sponsor instead. Dr. Bob is an example.

Some program members have spiritual advisors
in addition to their sponsors.

Is it possible to have more than one sponsor?

In theory, it is. The problem with a dual-sponsor arrangement is the temptation to play one sponsor against the other. A sponsee may seek different suggestions from each sponsor and choose the one he or she prefers as a rationalization for action or inaction.

Sponsorship creates an honest, intimate, trusting relationship built up over time that serves a single purpose: to help us stay sober by working the Twelve Steps and applying their principles in all our affairs. If we have that kind of relationship with a sponsor, we won't need more than one. Sponsorship is not the same as friendship, although it has some of the elements of friendship. As has been said, "I have lots of friends, but only one sponsor."

Before choosing a second sponsor, examine your motives. Has your sponsor moved to another town? Has your sponsor's life changed in such a way that he or she is no longer available (traveling more or new family responsibilities)? Are you thinking of changing sponsors and you want to give the new one a try before leaving the other one? These reasons may be valid for considering a second sponsor. Members with long-term sponsors often keep those sponsors when they or their sponsors move to another town. They may then get a second sponsor in the same town, however. (See the answer to the following question.)

Examine your motives for wanting a second sponsor.

On the other hand, are you taking on a second sponsor to create confusion or to avoid having to do the hard work your primary sponsor is pushing? Are you trying to hide by telling parts of your story to different sponsors, but not showing anyone the complete picture? Are you looking for an easier, softer way? These reasons are poor ones for choosing a second sponsor.

Can someone who lives in a different town sponsor me?

There is a difference of opinion on this issue. I don't recommend out-of-town sponsorship, except for long-term sponsorships, and even then I wonder about the desirability of it. My own belief is that each of us needs a sponsor in our hometown. We can have our long-term sponsor in another town if we want to continue to work with him or her (and many of us do), but we ought to have another sponsor in the same town.

It's better to have a sponsor who lives in the same town.

The reasons for choosing an in-town sponsor when our old sponsor has moved away (or we have) are many. Some of them are

1. We need to physically meet with our sponsors regularly. A lot is communicated in person that cannot be communicated over the telephone.
2. It is difficult to work the Steps with someone who is not physically present. Certain Steps, in fact, require a sponsor and sponsee to be together. This problem is not as great for old-timers who have been through the Twelve Steps as it is for newcomers. But it is still a problem because we never cease working the Steps.

No matter how long we have been in recovery,
we never stop working the Steps.

3. Sometimes a fresh look at ourselves is beneficial. With a new sponsor, we get that new look as well as a new perspective on the program.
4. When we get a new sponsor, we review the Twelve Steps and how we have worked them. This review can help us in pinpointing areas that need work.
5. We are not so "special" that only one sponsor in the world is right for us. We need to be willing to go through the process of opening ourselves up again to another human being.

How do I "fire" a sponsor?

The most courteous way to change sponsors is to discuss the change with your sponsor and discuss the reasons for it. Here are some of the reasons people have for changing sponsors:

- They identify some basic incompatibility with their sponsors (such as a personality clash or intolerance).
- They outgrow their sponsors.
- Their sponsors become possessive or controlling.
- Their sponsors do something that betrays their trust (such as reveal a confidence or try to take advantage of them in some way).
- Either they or their sponsors move to another town.
- They find someone with whom they think they can work more effectively.

The most productive way to "fire" a sponsor
is to confront the sponsor directly.

If you are changing sponsors because of something negative about your sponsor, make an appointment to discuss your reasons for changing. By doing so, you will help your sponsor examine his or her own behavior. You will also get to practice being honest and living up to your responsibilities. Regardless of what your sponsor has done lately, he or she has been of help to you in the past. You owe your sponsor the courtesy of saying good-bye and of formally releasing him or her from the sponsorship role.

If you don't have the courage to formally end the relationship, you can, of course, simply not call your sponsor anymore. This method is not recommended. Ultimately, a good sponsor will confront you on this behavior, and the issue will come to a head anyway. But the ending may be less satisfactory.

Why do I need a sponsor if I've been in recovery a long time?

No matter how long you've been clean, sober, or abstinent you never stop working the Steps. And you need another person to help you work the Steps, even when you're an old-timer.

There are other reasons, too. Twelve Step programs are based on staying clean, sober, or abstinent one day at a time. In one sense, nobody has more than a day of recovery; we are all just one drink, one drug, or one behavior away from a slip. No matter how long we have been in recovery, we still need someone to talk things over with. We still need that experience, strength, and hope that keeps us applying the Twelve Steps and living by their principles.

We never outgrow our need for a sponsor.

Aren't you asking somebody for a big favor to sponsor you?

It isn't a favor that you're asking. Sponsoring is one of the ways in which program members stay in recovery, so it is both a privilege and a necessity for us. Although it may not seem so to the newcomer, a sponsor gets as much out of the relationship as a sponsee—maybe more. Therefore, most program members want to sponsor new people, unless they already have as many sponsees as they can handle. Don't let your fear of being a burden on somebody keep you from finding a sponsor. Many of us consider the opportunity to sponsor someone a priceless gift.

Sponsorship is a privilege with many rewards.

Is it okay to ask a high-profile person to sponsor me?

Yes, but only if you are asking that person because it is the quality of his or her recovery that you admire. If you have some other motive, don't ask. It is not your sponsor's responsibility to get you a job, improve your social life, boost your career, or add to your prestige. If your real reason for asking the famous person to sponsor you is to take advantage of that fame in any way, then the relationship is doomed from the beginning.

When dealing with a high-profile sponsor, you have a special need to guard that person's anonymity. You have no right to reveal to anyone who your sponsor is or what your sponsor tells you. If you can't keep his or her identity a secret—even within the program—as well as what he or she says, you have no right to ask that person to sponsor you.

Check your motives before asking
a high-profile person to sponsor you.

Why can't I sponsor myself?

Because your best thinking got you to the program. We all need another perspective on our lives. Sponsorship provides that perspective, and it also builds humility. Even more important, the Steps cannot be worked alone, and the Steps are the basis of our recovery.

We can't sponsor ourselves.

What if my sponsor slips?

If your sponsor uses or drinks, find a new one immediately. A sponsor can only help you work the Steps that he or she has worked. A sponsor who uses or drinks has not worked the First Step.

It is always traumatic to lose a good friend to active addiction, and it is even more so when that friend is your sponsor. You may wish to increase your meetings as you adjust to the shock. Keep in mind that your own recovery is dependent upon the program and your Higher Power, not on your sponsor. Even though your sponsor's slip is frightening and painful, it does not endanger your recovery.

There shouldn't be any gurus in Twelve Step programs because we are all only one slip away from active addiction. For that reason and others, it's risky to put anyone in the program on a pedestal, including a sponsor. None of us belongs there and none of us does well there. Sponsors are special people to us, but, like all alcoholics or addicts, they have clay feet. They do sometimes drink or use again.

If your sponsor slips, find another one.

Is it okay to attend another Twelve Step group as well?

That decision is yours to make. There are some important considerations to take into account, however.

If you are dually addicted to alcohol and other drugs, for example, it makes sense to attend a Twelve Step program for drugs (such as Narcotics Anonymous or Cocaine Anonymous) at the same time that you are attending AA. AA's knowledge and experience is limited to alcohol, and it makes no claims about its ability to help someone recover from any other addiction. The same principle holds for other Twelve Step Fellowships which also restrict their experience to the addiction they were founded to relieve.

How do I pay back my sponsor for what he or she has done for me?

By being a good sponsor yourself. There is no other way we can repay our sponsors even though, in their own way, they have gotten as much out of the relationship as we have. It would be inappropriate and unacceptable to offer a sponsor money or anything else as a form of repayment. We act as sponsors because it is our responsibility to do so as Twelve Step members, not for any monetary gain.

We pay back our sponsors
by being the best sponsor we can be to someone else.

4

Some Questions Sponsees Ask about Their Sponsors

This chapter contains a group of questions that sponsees sometimes ask about their sponsors. The answers are based on my own experience and on consultations with other Twelve Step members whose recovery I respect. Not all program members will agree with the answers.

Do I have to take the Fifth Step with my sponsor?

No, you do not, but there should be a good reason for not doing so. The Fifth Step is an opportunity for your sponsor to get to know you well and for you to make yourself vulnerable to someone important to you. Since some of the information in the Fifth Step will resurface in the Ninth Step, your sponsor will have an advantage if he or she has heard your Fifth Step. Also, because your sponsor knows you, he or she will be able to recognize patterns in your behavior that warrant discussion in this Step.

If you don't want your sponsor to hear your Fifth Step because you don't trust your sponsor to keep your confidences or because you think that he or she will judge you, consider finding another sponsor. It's important to develop trust in someone else, and your sponsor is a likely candidate. That's one of the reasons he or she *is* your sponsor.

On the other hand, there may be some information that you need to omit from a Fifth Step with your sponsor. Conversations between a sponsor and sponsee are *not* considered "privileged" communications (information that is legally protected from being revealed to third parties) in the way that confidential disclosures to doctors and lawyers are. Therefore, if you have information that could be seriously damaging, you may wish to reserve that part of your Fifth Step for a clergy person with whom the information will be safe.

The AA Twelve and Twelve states, "It may turn out, however, that you'll choose someone else [other than your sponsor] for the more difficult and deeper revelations. This individual may be entirely outside of A.A.—for example, your clergyman or your doctor."[1] Having legally sensitive information in a Fourth Step is not an excuse for avoiding a Fifth Step. It merely changes the person who will hear all or part of that Step.

> *Most sponsees take the Fifth Step with their sponsors,*
> *but it isn't required that they do so.*

What if I can't reach my sponsor when I need him or her?

Call someone else you know in the program, or someone you don't know. Sponsors are important to us, but they have no special powers. Like other program members, they can only share their experience, strength, and hope. In an emergency, any program member can do the same.

Carry a list of Twelve Step members' telephone numbers in your wallet or purse to use in an emergency. If you don't have a list with you, call the Intergroup or Central Office in your community if you're in AA, or its equivalent if you're in another Twelve Step Fellowship. If necessary, call New York City or some other city where the office is likely to be open late. These telephone numbers are often available from directory assistance.

> *If you can't get hold of your sponsor in an emergency,*
> *call anyone in the program.*

Do I have to do what my sponsor says?

No, but you might want to consider why you are resisting the suggestion he or she has to offer. If you think your sponsor is wrong, tell him or her so and discuss the issue.

Sponsorship styles vary significantly from person to person. Some sponsors are more strict than others; some are more inclined to offer advice, make demands, or give orders. For some people new to recovery, being told what to do may work. For others, it does not. If your problem with your sponsor stems from his or her style rather than from one or two specific suggestions, discuss this issue. If your sponsor's style is to tell you what to do rather than offer suggestions or share his or her experience, strength, and hope, you have a right to bring this observation up. While your sponsor may guide your recovery program, it is not his or her responsibility to run your life. (See the answer to the following two questions.)

What if my sponsor is overprotective and wants to run my life?

Confront the overprotection by discussing it with your sponsor. If he or she agrees with you and is willing to do something about it, you have strengthened the relationship. If he or she does not agree with you and you're convinced you are right, then you may want to find another sponsor. A sponsor's behavior that might have been appropriate in the early days of your recovery may not be as effective for you later on, but be sure that your analysis of the situation is correct. Don't rationalize yourself into leaving a beneficial relationship in order to escape facing an issue or doing some hard work.

*Control issues may be a problem
with some sponsors*

What if I don't agree with my sponsor?

You will not always agree with your sponsor about his or her interpretation of the program. When the disagreement centers on an issue that can be resolved by referring to Conference-approved literature, go to those sources and read the relevant passages. If it's a matter of opinion that is not covered in Conference-approved literature, you and your sponsor can try to hammer out an agreement if the issue is important to the relationship. If it isn't or if you can't reach agreement, accept that you are each entitled to hold your own opinion. I don't agree with my sponsor on a number of recovery issues that are not critical to the sponsorship.

> *Disagreements about program principles can be resolved by referring to Conference-approved literature.*

If the disagreement concerns your character defects, attitudes, behavior, or personal problems, listen carefully. Often our sponsors will see something about us that we don't want to see ourselves. If we keep our minds open, later we may agree with our sponsors.

Even the most knowledgeable and experienced sponsors, however, have blind spots that can lead them astray. Sponsors tend to focus on issues that are important to them since that is where their experience, strength, and hope lie. Occasionally, a sponsor may try to focus a sponsee's attention on an issue that is an issue for the sponsor, but not for the sponsee. Or the sponsor may project his or her life experiences onto a sponsee so that only those experiences which parallel the sponsor's are acknowledged as valid. If you believe that your sponsor is discounting your own experience or that he or she is trying to focus your attention on an issue that is not an issue for you, confront your sponsor. It is important to bring this issue out into the open where it can be dealt with. Don't hide it. If you cannot satisfactorily resolve this serious problem, you may want to find another sponsor.

What if my sponsor won't return my phone calls?

If you are disturbed about your sponsor's telephone response rate, discuss the matter. But first, ask yourself: (1) Are my sponsor's reasons for not returning my telephone calls legitimate? (2) Am I making unreasonable demands on my sponsor's time? (3) Has the response rate changed?

Confronting the issue and looking for a solution is more productive than ignoring it or casting silent or public blame. One of the functions of sponsorship is to help you practice more effective behavior. Talking with your sponsor about the problem of the telephone calls is the kind of behavior you are trying to learn.

When a problem arises with your sponsor,
discuss it with him or her.

My sponsor told somebody else a secret about me. Now what?

You have to decide whether or not you can trust your sponsor again. We all make mistakes. Breaking a confidence is one of the worst mistakes a sponsor can make, however. If your sponsor has come to you about it and has made amends, you have to determine where you stand in the relationship. If you can put it behind you, you may wish to continue where you left off.

On the other hand, you have a right to aggressively protect your expectation of confidentiality on the part of your sponsor. Confidentiality is a *right* of sponsorship. It is the foundation on which a successful sponsorship relationship is built. We have to be able to trust our sponsors and feel safe with them in order to share our lives with them. If your confidence has been violated, consider changing sponsors. Losing you as a sponsee may be the consequence your sponsor needs in order to learn his or her lesson. If you believe that the breach of confidence was not a one-time mistake, but an ongoing risk, change sponsors immediately.

Replace your sponsor if he or she
cannot keep your confidences.

My sponsor keeps taking my inventory.
What do I do about that?

It depends on what you mean by "taking my inventory." If you mean that your sponsor helps you identify the character defects that cause you problems and suggests that you apply specific Steps to eliminate them, your sponsor is doing his or her job. If, on the other hand, you mean that your sponsor is focused on listing your faults without bringing the Steps or program principles to bear on removing them, the relationship is troubled. However, be careful that you are not projecting your own feelings onto your sponsor. It is easy, especially in early recovery, to be confused about what we are feeling and why.

What if I have outgrown my sponsor?

Find a new one. It is possible that sometime in your recovery, you will make more progress than your sponsor and will outgrow him or her. To outgrow someone means to get ahead of that person in the program so that he or she is no longer able to help you make further progress. Having worked more Steps than your sponsor is an example. So is developing a greater maturity or being more willing to give up resentments or living in the solution while your sponsor is still in the problem. You will know when your sponsor is no longer helping you move forward.

If you outgrow your sponsor, find another one.

What if I dread calling my sponsor?

If your dread is the rare experience occasioned by having to admit a wrong, make an amend, or own up to not having worked the program, it is part of sponsorship. If it results from being new to the program and not yet accustomed to making that daily telephone call to a new sponsor, it's part of the process. On the other hand, if it is an ongoing dread that it is not relieved by the call itself, there may be a problem in the relationship. Some sponsors shame their sponsees rather than support them within a tough-love framework. If your sponsor is shaming you, but won't admit it, or if you cannot figure out what the dread is about and cannot resolve it, find a second sponsor and see if it continues with him or her. Your work with a sponsor should not be characterized by dreading contact with him or her.

What if my sponsor dumps on me?

Some sponsors use their sponsees as a dumping ground for emotions they don't want to deal with and need to get rid of. They dump those feelings on the sponsee who then feels worse than when the conversation started. If your sponsor is more interested in talking about himself or herself than about you, and if you routinely feel worse after talking to him or her, ask yourself if you're being emotionally dumped on. For example, if your sponsor says regularly, "You think you've had a bad day. Listen to this...," it may be a sign of discounting your feelings while dumping his or hers. If you confront your sponsor on the practice and it continues, you may want to find another sponsor.

As sponsees, we should not be dumping grounds
for our sponsors' unwanted emotions.

What if my sponsor tries to force his or her religious beliefs on me?

A Twelve Step program is not a religious program. It is contrary to Twelve Step tradition for sponsors to try to convert their sponsees to their own religious beliefs (or for sponsees to try to do the same with their sponsors, as sometimes happens). The basis of Twelve Step spirituality is acknowledgment of the validity of each person's interpretation of "God as we understand God." That interpretation depends entirely upon the individual, even if it means no God at all.

It is inappropriate, therefore, for either the sponsor or sponsee to try to convert the other to a set of specific religious beliefs. Confront your sponsor on this practice, and ask him or her to stop. If he or she is unable to do so, find another sponsor.

What do I do if my sponsor stops working his or her program?

Confront your sponsor. Sponsorship is a two-way street. The relationship you have built up is probably as important to your sponsor as it is to you. This is an opportunity for you to help your sponsor because of your intimate knowledge of his or her character and behavior. When Bill Wilson went on a major dry drunk, he was confronted by fellow AA members who knew him well.

You might also call your grandsponsor (your sponsor's sponsor) and talk to him or her about it. If the problem continues for an extended period of time and is interfering with the sponsorship relationship, consider finding a temporary sponsor. When a lapse in working the program renders your sponsor unable to assist you with the Steps, you need someone who can provide the necessary guidance for you to continue working them.

Confront your sponsor if he or she stops working the program.

What if I find out my sponsor hasn't been honest with me?

It depends upon what your sponsor hasn't been honest about. If your sponsor has lied about something related directly to the program, such as his or her recovery date or the Steps worked, or has lied in an effort to persuade you to do something you would not have done had you known the truth, find another sponsor. If you believe that your sponsor is a chronic liar, find one who isn't. Honesty is the basis of all Twelve Step programs. It is what you are trying to learn. You can't learn it from a dishonest sponsor, although it is the Steps and not a sponsor who will ultimately teach you to be honest.

On the other hand, if you are new to the sponsorship and your sponsor's secret is a deep one unrelated to the program, it may be that he or she felt it was too soon to reveal it. You will have to make the judgment call.

What if my sponsor or I want to bring up issues from other Twelve Step Fellowships?

There are several factors to consider in answering this question. They are (1) your length of recovery from your primary addiction, (2) the nature of the other Twelve Step group, and (3) who is bringing up the other issues.

In general, it is better in the first year of recovery to focus exclusively on your primary addiction. However, if you are addicted to more than one psychoactive chemical (such as to alcohol and other drugs), you may need to join another Twelve Step Fellowship to deal with both the alcohol and drug addiction. If your secondary addiction does not involve psychoactive drugs but is so out of control that it may lead you back to your primary addiction or otherwise cause serious damage in your life, you may have to join another Twelve Step Fellowship to deal with that problem as well. On the other hand, if it is possible to focus just on your primary addiction in the first year, it is better to do so.

In later years, you can turn your attention to the other issues creating problems in your life. The idea of restricting your focus to your most urgent addiction or addictions is that many other problems will clear up with recovery from that addiction. In addition, it requires great attention and effort to apply Twelve Step principles to your primary addiction. Other Twelve Step group memberships may distract you from that task.

Remember that your sponsor is only qualified to help you work the Twelve Steps in the Fellowship of which he or she is a member. While you may wish to discuss other issues, compulsions, or addictions with your sponsor as they impact your primary recovery, you cannot expect your sponsor to help you with them as he or she would with your primary addiction. If you are in another Twelve Step Fellowship, you probably have a sponsor to help you work the Steps of that program.

If it is your sponsor who raises the other Twelve Step group issues because he or she is pushing his or her own codependency, compulsion, or addiction issues onto you, discuss the problem. You have asked your sponsor to help you with your primary addiction program. You have a right to restrict his or her guidance to that area.

PART II

*Being
a Sponsor*

5

Sponsorship Expectations

Perhaps the greatest potential source of misunderstanding between a sponsor and a sponsee is the different expectations each has for the sponsorship relationship. The sponsor views sponsorship in one way, and the sponsee views it in another way. When the relationship doesn't turn out the way each wanted it to, they are both disappointed. To prevent this situation from developing, we have a responsibility to discuss our understanding—and the potential sponsee's understanding—of the sponsorship role.

Our first responsibility to a potential sponsee
is to discuss our mutual expectations for the sponsorship.

As a potential sponsor, we are saying, in effect, "This is how I sponsor somebody. If this is not what you are expecting from me, then we need to discuss whether or not we can work together as sponsor and sponsee." To adequately cover this area, we need to discuss the following issues with a potential sponsee:

- *Our mutual understanding of sponsorship.* What does our potential sponsee think it is? What do we think it is?
- *Our mutual expectations for the sponsorship.* What does our potential sponsee want from us? What do we expect from him or her? What are our obligations and responsibilities to each other?

· *Why our potential sponsee is changing sponsors (if the sponsee is not a newcomer).* Since behavioral patterns tend to repeat themselves, explore the reasons for the change. What was the source of the potential sponsee's dissatisfaction with his or her former sponsor? What does the potential sponsee expect from us that he or she did not get from the previous sponsor?

**If we discuss our mutual expectations at the beginning,
the sponsorship will go more smoothly.**

This chapter provides a checklist of some common expectations between sponsors and sponsees. We may have other expectations that are unique to us as sponsors, and we should discuss them as well. Our expectations reflect, to some degree, our style of sponsorship. If our potential sponsee is not comfortable with that style, we are better off finding out now. Or if our potential sponsee is not willing to follow the basic ground rules we intend to set, we should know that too. If we decide that the match between us is a good one, we can proceed with the sponsorship. If we decide that it is not, we will save both of us a lot of pain by declining the sponsorship opportunity.

**Our goal in interviewing a potential sponsee
is to determine how well we will work together.**

Each sponsee is different. An approach that is effective with one sponsee may not be effective with another. And what may be effective in the first months of recovery may not be effective in the first years. We have to meet our sponsees' needs as they exist at the moment, because those needs will change as our sponsees grow in the program. We have to be willing to let our sponsees change and grow—and even grow away.

In the special case of opposite-sex sponsorships, same-sex homosexual sponsorships, and same-sex gay/straight sponsorships, an additional step is required in the interview process. Sponsors and sponsees develop an intimate and trusting relationship with one another. In such an environment of acceptance and vulnerability (and love), it is possible for sexual feelings to develop. To guard against problems arising from that development, certain precautions should be taken from the beginning. These precautions include the following:

1. Ask yourself if your potential sponsee may have a romantic or sexual interest in you that is motivating the sponsorship request. If it is appropriate, ask your potential sponsee that question. Ask yourself the same question regarding your inclination to accept. If any answer is yes, don't sponsor the person.
2. Consider discussing the risk that sexual feelings might develop and agree to terminate the sponsorship if they do.
3. If sexual feelings do develop, break off the sponsorship and cease sponsorship activities (stop working the Steps together and so on). Then
   · Suggest that your sponsee find another sponsor as quickly as possible, using a temporary sponsor if necessary. The temporary sponsor should be told about the situation.
   · Begin a "cooling-off" period in which contact between the two of you is broken.

The last suggestion may sound harsh, but if the attraction is based on real love and not on dependency associated with sponsorship, it will survive this break. While the action may not be pleasant for either party, it is the price to be paid for the risk that was taken in the first place and the situation that developed.

The following is a list of common expectations that are often discussed with a new sponsee. Once these expectations have been discussed and agreed upon, they become the ground rules of the sponsorship.

SOME EXPECTATIONS TO CONSIDER
IN SPONSORSHIP

1. *Ethics*
2. *Confidentiality*
3. *Mutual honesty*
4. *Working the Steps*
5. *Meeting attendance*
6. *Sponsor availability*
7. *Frequency of contact*
8. *When and where to call*
9. *Sponsor replacement*
10. *Spirituality*

Ethics

Sponsorship is not a casual relationship with another person. It is a relationship carefully structured to serve a specific purpose within the program. It is, above all else, a sacred trust that we have accepted. It is not a burden, but a gift; and it carries specific responsibilities and obligations. The relationship between a sponsor and sponsee is never equal, although the mutual benefits may be. A sponsee is always vulnerable and subject to manipulation at the hands of a sponsor.

Sponsorship is a sacred trust.

It goes without saying that we should never try to exploit or take advantage of a sponsee in any way. Nor should we ever do anything that even suggests it. Sponsors and sponsees are not just friends, although there are elements of friendship involved. As sponsors, we are charged with helping our sponsees work the Twelve Steps and with guiding their recovery program based on the experience, strength, and hope of our own recovery. In many ways, they are our students.

Our special relationship with sponsees requires us to live by strict moral and ethical standards. We are never to do anything that would harm them in any way—physically, emotionally, spiritually, financially, intellectually, socially. We are not to use them as a way to make money, to borrow money, to have sex, to advance our careers, to improve our social status, or to get anything from them whatsoever for our own personal gain. If we cannot trust ourselves to live by these strict ethical standards, we should not sponsor them.

Confidentiality

The pledge of confidentiality between us and our sponsee is the basis of the trust we share. Our mutual promise not to repeat anything told in confidence opens the way to self-examination and self-revelation. We both have a right to the privacy of our lives. The confidentiality that I maintain for my sponsees covers all their lives, not just their secrets. The only exception I ask for, as sponsor, is permission to discuss my sponsee with my own sponsor whenever I believe it is in my sponsee's best interest for me to do so.

A sponsee's confidence must never be broken.

My level of confidentiality includes the identity of my sponsees. It's up to them, not me, to reveal that I am their sponsor. Such protection is warranted if my sponsee and I are to build a safe, long-term relationship. If someone asks me about an individual whom they know I sponsor, I simply tell them that I never discuss my sponsees with another person.

I advise my sponsees, however, that the confidences between us are not protected by law in the way that privileged information is between an attorney and a client or a priest and a parishioner. And sponsors do sometimes drink again. In addition, as sponsors, we have a legal obligation to report certain ongoing crimes (such as child abuse). Therefore, our sponsees should be careful in sharing certain information that could be seriously damaging to them. In such cases, I suggest they consider meeting with a clergy person or doctor for that portion of their Fifth Step when the time comes.

Mutual Honesty

Twelve Step recovery is based on the capacity to be honest, so honesty is one of the ground rules we discuss at the beginning of the sponsorship. Since many newcomers learn honesty while in the program, the goal is progress, not perfection. If your sponsee has a serious problem with being honest, honesty should be a focus of your work together. The Steps, if worked properly, will make us honest. In the meantime, I expect my sponsees to be honest about their drinking or drug use and about the basics of the program, including whether or not they are working the Steps. Honesty is a two-way street, and what is appropriate for our sponsees in this regard is also appropriate for us. As sponsors, we try to model honesty for our own sponsees, both self-honesty and honesty with others.

**Recovery is based on the capacity
to be honest.**

On the other hand, it isn't necessary for us to reveal everything to our sponsees at the beginning of the relationship just as it isn't necessary for them to reveal everything to us. We may both want to see how well the relationship works before we reveal our deepest secrets.

Working the Steps

The Steps form the basis of every Twelve Step recovery program. Other program activities (meetings, sponsors, and Conference-approved literature) are designed to support us in working the Steps. Since our primary function as sponsors is to help our sponsees work the Steps, we should emphasize their importance from the beginning. My expectation for each of my sponsees is that he will be willing to work the Twelve Steps, and I ask for that commitment before agreeing to sponsor him.

**Starting the Steps is a priority
for program newcomers.**

Meeting Attendance

For newcomers to Alcoholics Anonymous, the suggested meeting attendance is ninety meetings in ninety days. Such a rigorous meeting schedule gives newcomers a firm grounding in program principles and establishes a new behavioral pattern based on acceptance of their alcoholism. It also represents a commitment to sobriety and to the work it requires. Ninety meetings in ninety days can also be recommended for other Twelve Step programs to help newcomers reduce their loneliness and sense of isolation. For these reasons and more, many of us have the "ninety-in-ninety" expectation for our sponsees and make that commitment a condition of sponsorship.

I encourage my newcomer sponsees to include as many speaker meetings as possible in their ninety meetings. Speaker meetings help newcomers identify as alcoholics, addicts, or compulsive individuals. Speaker meetings also show newcomers that they can recover in a Twelve Step program and that they can be happy and successful. In speaker meetings, they get a full hour of experience, strength, and hope relating to recovery.

**Speaker meetings are especially good
for newcomers.**

Sponsor Availability

If our potential sponsee expects a lot of attention that we won't have the time to provide, we need to know that before we accept the sponsor role. Otherwise, problems will soon arise in the relationship. It is true that the degree of time we can make available to our sponsee changes, but there is an overall time availability that is characteristic of our style of sponsorship. Only by discussing this issue can we be sure that our expectation of availability matches our potential sponsee's expectation of contact.

Frequency of Contact

As a condition of sponsorship, I ask that a new sponsee call me every day for a specified number of days. In the case of a newcomer, it is ninety calls in ninety days to match his meeting attendance. I may limit the number of daily calls to thirty or sixty days for sponsees with more sobriety.

Ninety calls in ninety days
has many advantages for a newcomer.

There are several reasons why I ask a new sponsee to agree to this schedule:

· It is an expression of our mutual commitment to the sponsor/ sponsee relationship.
· It allows me to monitor his daily progress in the program which is especially important with newcomers.
· It is an expression of his willingness to work the program and an act of self-discipline that provides a model for other areas of his life.
· It allows me to get to know him quickly.
· It gives me the time I need with him to discuss program principles and their application to his life.
· It shows my sponsee how to break out of the loneliness and isolation of the addictive life by reaching out to another recovering person. "Reaching out" is not a natural reflex for most of us who are new to a Twelve Step program, and so we need the practice.
· It establishes a habit of regular contact that will continue throughout our relationship (although not daily later on).

The length of time spent on the telephone is not as important as the call itself. When sponsees don't have time to talk, they just check in, or they leave a message on the answering machine and fulfill their commitment that way.

When and Where to Call

It is important to discuss with our sponsees when and where it is appropriate for them to call us and for us to call them on a nonemergency basis. For example, is it okay to call each other at our workplaces? If so, during what hours? What kind of message should we leave? Is it okay to call at home and, if so, during what hours?

Most of us urge our sponsees to call us any time, day or night, if they are about to take a drink. In fact, it is crucial that they do so if the call is all that stands between them and a return to active addiction. I have a program friend who, upon agreeing to sponsor someone, hands her new sponsee twenty-five cents and says, "This is so you'll always have a quarter to call me if you need me. But call me *before* you drink."

**Set up ground rules for
telephone calls from your sponsee.**

Sponsor Replacement

Sponsees deserve to know that they are welcome to change sponsors whenever they want. I make this point clear in our first meeting.

Spirituality

The purpose of the Twelve Steps is to bring about a spiritual awakening. Since some of us are more spiritually oriented than others, our potential sponsees have a right to know the degree to which we will emphasize the spiritual aspect of the program as well as our level of tolerance for different religious or spiritual beliefs. If your interpretation of "God as we understand God" is no God at all, your potential sponsee should know that as well.

6

Some Questions Sponsors Ask about Sponsorship

This chapter contains questions that sponsors sometimes ask about Twelve Step sponsorship. The answers are based on my experience and on consultations with other program members whose recovery I respect. Your own sponsor will be a valuable resource in helping you answer these questions when they arise. Not all program members will agree with the answers.

What is my primary purpose as a sponsor?

Your primary purpose is to help your sponsee work the Twelve Steps. All your efforts and activities as a sponsor revolve around this central responsibility. Working the Steps is your sponsee's key to lasting recovery and to the fulfillment of the Promises.

What are the best suggestions I can offer my sponsees?

Don't drink or use. Go to meetings, read the Big Book or equivalent, work the Steps, say your prayers, and call your sponsor. Also, help another addicted person, and take life and recovery one day at a time.

How do the responsibilities of a temporary sponsor differ from those of a primary sponsor?

We have the same responsibilities to a temporary sponsee as to a "permanent" one. Because temporary sponsees are generally newcomers, temporary sponsorships tend to be intense and time-consuming.

Temporary sponsorships can be a big help to newcomers while they look for a primary sponsor.

The major difference between a temporary and primary sponsorship is that the temporary sponsorship is based on immediate need, and it is often without the thorough discussion that normally accompanies the selection of a primary sponsor. As a result, the difference in expectations between the sponsor and sponsee may be great, and the long-term match between the two may not be good. The relationship can certainly work for the short term, however, while the temporary sponsee looks for a primary sponsor and learns how to stay in recovery.

What do I tell my sponsees when they ask if they have to go to meetings for the rest of their lives?

There are at least two good answers. The first is the one-day-at-a-time answer. It is this: when we think about not drinking or using and "the rest of our lives," we are dealing with a very long time. Our Twelve Step program suggests that we think in terms of a much shorter period: one day at a time. Or even one hour at a time if necessary. If we stay clean and sober one day at a time, the rest of our lives will take care of themselves. Whether or not we will attend meetings for as long as we live is not a decision we have to make today if we are taking life and recovery one day at a time.

The second answer is this: although we don't have to think about the rest of our lives today, the truth is that there are no graduation ceremonies in Twelve Step programs. Recovery is a journey and not a destination. It is a process. We are never cured of our addiction. Experience indicates that those who continue to attend meetings have a better chance of staying clean, sober, or abstinent than those who do not. Since the price of a return to active addiction is potentially death, continuing to go to meetings is a reasonable choice. Those of us who have made that choice have found a bonus in it: our lives have continued to get richer and more enjoyable.

How many sponsees is too many?

It depends on your personality, the circumstances of your life, and your degree of preferred involvement with sponsees. It also depends upon how long your sponsees have been sober, since newcomers require more time and attention than mid-timers. Only you can decide. In making the decision, be fair to yourself as well as to your sponsees by not taking on so many that you short-change them.

Our grandiosity is easily fed by the attention of numerous sponsees so we have to be careful about having too many. I have known program members who compulsively collected sponsees and moved with an entourage from meeting to meeting. There is a limit to the number of sponsees we can work with effectively. It is a disservice to them and to ourselves if we develop a sponsee addiction.

The intensive work of sponsorship
restricts the number of sponsees we can handle comfortably.

What are the warning signs of a slip?

There are numerous warning signs of a slip. Some are subtle and some are not so subtle. When you get to know your sponsee well enough, you will know when he or she is off the beam. You may even know before your sponsee does. The exhibition of only one warning sign may not indicate trouble. For example, someone may cut back temporarily on his or her meetings for a good reason (frequent travel, for example). Or he or she may be cutting back from ninety meetings in ninety days after several months in the program.

Be alert to the warning signs
of a slip in your sponsees.

Nevertheless, each of the conditions listed below should be discussed with a sponsee when it occurs. In combination, they suggest a potential problem:

· Cutting down on meetings; cutting meetings out altogether is a very dangerous sign.
· Reassociating with old drinking or using friends.
· Returning to old drinking or using haunts.
· Seldom calling you, or not calling you at all.
· Forgetting how bad it was and focusing on how good some of the old times were in their drinking, using, or compulsive days.
· Abandoning prayer and meditation.
· Isolating themselves, especially from program friends.
· Complaining that meetings don't work anymore.
· Not working the Steps.

When is it appropriate for a sponsor to terminate a sponsorship relationship?

The termination of sponsorship is a grave matter that requires thought, prayer, and consultation with your own sponsor. There are situations in which it is warranted because it serves the best interests of both you and your sponsee. Some of the criteria that can be used to determine when a sponsorship relationship ought to be terminated are

1. If the relationship is endangering your own sobriety or seriously impairing your serenity *for whatever reason.* Your recovery always comes first.

*Terminate any sponsorship relationship
that is endangering your own recovery.*

2. If your sponsee outgrows you, and you think that he or she would make more progress with another sponsor.
3. If your sponsee refuses to work the Steps. It is very difficult to help a member of the Fellowship who won't work the Steps. You may prefer to spend your time on someone who is willing to work them, since helping your sponsee do so is your primary responsibility as a sponsor.
4. If the sponsee cannot or will not work on being honest with you and others about his or her life. Twelve Step Fellowships are programs of honesty. A sponsee who is not open to learning honesty is difficult to help. The truth is that a sponsee who is not willing to get honest is not willing to enter recovery.

   As with other guidelines, there are exceptions, particularly with newcomers who are, by nature, dishonest. It is progress, not perfection, that counts. If your sponsee is working hard at getting honest, that effort itself is a form of progress and honesty. If dishonesty is a major character defect of your sponsee, it should be a regular topic of discussion between the two of you, and something he or she is consciously working on.
5. Whenever anything happens that leads you to believe that the sponsorship is no longer in the best interests of your sponsee.

*Terminate any sponsorship relationship whenever it is
in the best interests of your sponsee to do so.*

How do I de-sponsor somebody?

By meeting your sponsee face to-face and telling him or her honestly why you are terminating the sponsor/sponsee relationship. It is important to model honest, responsible behavior in this process.

If the problem is with you (for example, if you are unable to keep a confidence), be honest about the specific problem. If amends are called for, make them forthrightly at this time. Concentrate on cleaning up your side of the street, and don't worry about your sponsee's.

If the problem is with your sponsee, deal with the issues matter-of-factly. You do not have to apologize for de-sponsoring someone. It was a privilege you extended, and you have a right to withdraw it. However, you owe it to your sponsee to explain clearly why you are terminating the sponsorship. Only then can your sponsee learn from his or her mistakes and fully understand the consequences of the inappropriate behavior.

What if I make a mistake?

Congratulations, you're human. Promptly admit it in accordance with Step Ten, "Continued to take personal inventory and when we were wrong promptly admitted it." If amends are due, make them. Learn from the mistake. And go on.

How soon can I sponsor somebody?

There are no rules about when you can sponsor somebody, and there would be exceptions if there were rules. Nevertheless, some general guidelines that are probably good for both you and your prospective sponsee are listed below. Not every program member will agree with them.

You are probably ready to sponsor someone when you have met *all* the following criteria:

1. You have a solid foundation in your program, which usually means a minimum of one year of continuous recovery.
2. You have a sponsor yourself.
3. You have worked *at least* the first five Steps.

4. You have read the major Conference-approved literature or your Fellowship's basic texts (the Big Book, the Twelve and Twelve, NA's Basic Text, and so on).
5. You attend meetings regularly.
6. You are working the Steps.

We earn the privilege of sponsoring someone
after we have passed certain milestones.

If your sponsee gets ahead of you in working the Steps, you should resign as his or her sponsor. Since your primary responsibility is to help your sponsee work the Steps, and since "you cannot give away what you don't have," you can't help him or her with the Steps you haven't worked. Theory is not enough. You have to actually have worked the Steps yourself to guide your sponsee through them.

How do I treat a high-profile sponsee such as a politician or an actor?

The same way you would treat somebody who was not famous. In fact, it's crucial that you treat your high-profile sponsee that way. One of the problems for celebrities who are trying to recover is that they are likely to receive special treatment that indulges their fantasies and their grandiosity. Celebrities are like everyone else, except they are famous. They are just as likely to be ungrateful, angry, depressed, on the pity pot, and self-centered as the rest of us. What they need in a sponsor is someone who will call them on their inappropriate behavior and addictive thinking. They need the same discipline and tough love as everybody else in the program.

When dealing with a high-profile sponsee, *always* protect his or her anonymity. Never break it to anyone. It is nobody's business inside of the program or outside of the program whom you sponsor. You have no right to tell anyone that you are sponsoring a famous person, much less tell anything that the person has told you. If you are not capable of keeping your famous sponsee's identity completely confidential, then you should refuse to sponsor that person. Not being able to brag about your sponsee is the price you pay for sponsoring him or her.

Celebrity sponsees need tough love
and protected anonymity.

One other requirement for sponsoring high-profile people is being willing not to take advantage of them. If you cannot resist the temptation to ask them to help you sell a movie script, find a job, influence a piece of legislation, get you a coveted ticket, arrange an invitation to a party, set up an introduction, and so on, you have no business sponsoring them. It is a betrayal of the sponsorship relationship to ask high-profile sponsees to do anything other than to work their programs to the best of their abilities.

Should I offer to sponsor someone?

Absolutely, as long as you're comfortable making the offer and it's followed with, "When you want another sponsor, you're welcome to find one." This approach works best on a temporary basis since it's difficult to tell whether or not a sponsorship will work in the long term without a discussion of mutual expectations. This offer can be a great blessing for newcomers who haven't mustered enough courage to ask someone to sponsor them. Once they've had a temporary sponsor, it's easier for them to find a primary sponsor later.

An offer to sponsor someone can introduce sponsorship
to a newcomer who is afraid to ask.

With whom can I discuss my sponsee's problem?

Only with his or her grandsponsor (i.e., with your own sponsor) unless you have his or her express permission to do otherwise.

The confidentiality that you must maintain between you and your sponsee prohibits you from talking about your sponsee's problem with anyone else inside or outside the program.

Is it okay to assign readings to a sponsee for discussion?

Yes. In fact, it's a good idea to give reading assignments to your sponsee. Assignments in the Big Book or equivalent and in other Conference-approved literature can familiarize your sponsee with the program and provide a specific topic for the two of you to discuss. Making an assignment has the added advantage of getting you to do the reading yourself.

*Reading assignments are good
for both you and your sponsee.*

Is it okay to give sponsees assignments other than readings?

It is, in my opinion, if the assignment is offered in the following way. I tell my sponsee that I want to give him an assignment because I believe that it will help him in his recovery. I explain what the assignment is and why I think it will help. I ask him if he is willing to accept the assignment. If he is not, I ask him why not, but then I let it go. If he accepts the assignment, I ask him to make a commitment to keep it. If he does not keep it, we discuss why he hasn't. The advantage of this approach is that it keeps me from telling my sponsees what to do.

Most of the time, the assignments I give a sponsee are for fixed terms, and they are designed to illustrate some character defect or to help him practice a Twelve Step principle or new behavior.

*Temporary action assignments
for sponsees can help them practice Twelve Step principles.*

How far do I have to go to keep a sponsee in recovery?

You never keep a sponsee in recovery! You are not responsible for anyone's recovery but your own. Neither are you responsible for anybody's slip but your own. It is easy to get caught up in our own grandiosity and think that we are keeping our sponsees in recovery. We are not. As AA says, "We don't get sponsees sober; we don't get them drunk." Another AA slogan that fits is, "We carry the message, not the alcoholic." Sponsees keep themselves in recovery through their program, the Twelve Steps, and their Higher Power. This concept of a sponsee's responsibility for his or her own recovery is essential to maintaining our own humility. It also takes a great burden off our shoulders.

It is never our responsibility to keep sponsees in recovery. That's their job.

When am I enabling a sponsee?

Whenever you try to do a sponsee's work for him or her, that's enabling. Enabling is trying to provide an "easier, softer way" for a sponsee or trying to protect a sponsee from reality, from legitimate pain, from the consequences of his or her actions, or from the hard work of the program. Whenever we enable by making decisions for our sponsees or doing for them what they should be doing for themselves, we are taking away their autonomy and undermining their recovery. Enabling in all its forms is against Twelve Step principles.

How do I handle relationships among my sponsees?

Although not every program member will agree with this answer, I believe in keeping my sponsees separate from each other. I never mention one sponsee to another. I never reveal their names or their activities. And I never take them anywhere together as a group. If my sponsees figure out who their fellow sponsees are, that's okay, but I don't tell them. (At one time I did tell my existing sponsees when I took on a new one, but I no longer think that's a good policy.) I believe strongly in this separation of sponsees for several reasons:

- It strengthens our humility. Our grandiosity is easily fed by being surrounded by an entourage of sponsees. Sponsees are not trophies to our recovery.
- It eliminates the potential development of "sibling rivalry" among sponsees. It is easy for sponsees to become jealous of one another over the amount of time and attention paid to them in relation to their fellow sponsees.
- It prevents us from intentionally or unintentionally playing favorites with our sponsees or pitting one against the other for our own selfish ends.

Some sponsors prefer to be with only one sponsee at a time.

What can I recommend to a sponsee as a substitute for a Twelve Step meeting?

There is no substitute for a Twelve Step meeting. When your sponsee is feeling squirrelly, it may help to read one of the story chapters in the Big Book or equivalent or something from other program literature. Prayer and meditation, calling another member of the Fellowship, making a gratitude list, applying the appropriate Step, or working with another addicted person may also provide relief.

Reading a personal story in the Big Book or equivalent is an antidote to feeling squirrelly.

What should I tell a newcomer sponsee about thirteenth stepping?

There is no thirteenth step. The phrase is used to mean making inappropriate sexual advances toward a person in the Fellowship, such as a sponsor approaching a sponsee or an established member approaching a member with less than a year of recovery.

During the first twelve months of recovery, it is suggested that members of the Fellowship not involve themselves in "romantic entanglements" (an old AA euphemism for sexual affairs) while they go about the business of stabilizing their recovery. The reason for this suggestion is that a sexual affair diverts the newcomer from his or her primary purpose of staying in recovery; may encourage that newcomer to transfer his or her dependence to the new love object rather than to the Twelve Steps; raises all kinds of emotions that the newcomer is not prepared to deal with; and is likely to lead the newcomer back to active addiction.

For these reasons, and because of the emotional vulnerability that makes new members easy targets for manipulation, thirteenth stepping is unacceptable. It is a betrayal of the program's safe and trusting atmosphere. Thirteenth stepping is predatory behavior that corrupts the Twelve Step program's primary purpose of helping people recover.

Thirteenth stepping refers to making sexual advances toward someone inappropriate, such as a program newcomer.

Unfortunately, there are members of both sexes who prey on newcomers and the emotionally vulnerable. Newcomer sponsees should be warned about this possibility. As a rule, the men or women who romantically interest your sponsees in their first months or year of recovery will no longer interest them in their second or third years. They will have changed too much as a result of their progress in the Fellowship.

In the first year of our sobriety, most of us have little to offer emotionally. So those with substantial recovery time who come on to newcomers sexually have a problem. Or an objective. Perhaps they are looking for sex without emotional commitment (often a prelude to being dumped). Or perhaps they are taking advantage of the newcomers' emotional vulnerability because they can't compete when the playing field is level. Perhaps they are so emotionally stunted themselves that only a newcomer will find them attractive and vice versa. Whatever the reason, they are bad news for your sponsee.

Even so, your sponsee may choose to get sexually involved with someone from the program during the first year of recovery. The choice is his or hers to make. All you can do is try to keep your sponsee focused on the Steps and the hard work that needs to be done in the program. You can tell him or her, "This may be the love of your life, but if it isn't and it comes to be a bad end, don't slip."

Warn your sponsee against thirteenth stepping.
It is unacceptable behavior in Twelve Step programs.

What is the greatest danger in sponsorship?

I'm not sure what the greatest danger is, but a significant one is sponsor possessiveness. It isn't just a control problem. It's the kind of possessiveness that keeps a sponsee from growing, from making his or her own decisions and mistakes, and from becoming his or her own person. I have seen sponsors who became so possessive of their sponsees that they act like jealous lovers.

Such sponsors want to embed themselves in their sponsees' lives, controlling their decisions and keeping them dependent. These sponsors are bitterly disappointed when their sponsees leave them, generally after a year or so. "I did so much for them!" they complain. "How could they have left me like that?" The answer is to save themselves.

Be careful about possessiveness and control. If you work well with sponsees in the early days of their recovery, but not later on, and they leave you with bitterness, look at your side of the street. What do you need to change about yourself? What does this pattern tell you about your ego and your need to control? Our goal in working with sponsees is to help them grow up and find "a new freedom"—not to imprison them.

7

Some Questions Sponsors Ask about Their Sponsees

This chapter contains questions sponsors sometimes ask about their sponsees. The answers are based on my experience and on consultations with other Twelve Step members whose recovery I respect. Your own sponsor will be a valuable resource in helping you answer these questions. Not all program members will agree with the answers.

What if my sponsee doesn't do what I tell him or her to do?

As sponsors, we are to share our experience, strength, and hope with our sponsees rather than tell them what to do. Even the Twelve Steps are "suggested." Sponsees deserve to make the basic decisions about their lives including whether or not to work their program or to stay in recovery. As their sponsors, we are entitled to suggest, but not to dictate. One of our responsibilities is to prepare our sponsees to be accountable and responsible for their own behavior. We can't accomplish that objective if we are telling them what to do. They have a right to their own mistakes and to the lessons they will learn from them.

As sponsors, we share our experience, strength, and hope
with our sponsees rather than tell them what to do.

Not everyone in a Twelve Step program would agree that sponsees are not to be told what to do in the early days of their recovery. I hold to the idea that how they live their lives is always their decision and I should not be deciding for them. To do so creates an unhealthy dependency. It *is* up to me, however, to help them see, realistically, the alternatives they have. Newcomers frequently have trouble sorting out alternatives. I will help them do that, and I will bring Twelve Step principles and experience to bear on the issue, but I will not make the decision itself no matter how much they plead or how much I want to. When they ask, "What would you do if you were me?" I answer quite genuinely, "I don't know, because I'm not you." I am willing to tell them what I believe program experience suggests, but I always leave the final decision to them.

We feed our grandiosity
when we try to run our sponsees' lives.

How do I handle it when my sponsee has another sponsor who disagrees with me?

It's unusual for a sponsee to have multiple sponsors. However, if your sponsee is getting conflicting suggestions from another sponsor, try to help your sponsee sort out the alternatives, bringing Twelve Step principles and wisdom to bear. The decision is your sponsee's. If you are not heavily invested in whether or not your sponsee does what you think is best, it won't matter as much.

What do I do when my sponsee lies to me?

Confront the sponsee immediately. A Twelve Step program is one of honesty, and honesty is something we're trying to teach our sponsees. If you and your sponsee are not developing increasing trust and honesty with each other, the sponsorship is in jeopardy. Honesty is one of the ground rules. However, I don't expect a new sponsee to reveal everything at once regarding the past and certain issues in the present, nor do I reveal all my private issues. As trust builds between us, we are each more willing to share our secrets with the other.

Newcomer sponsees fall into a special category. Very often they don't know *how* to be honest, so the approach with them is different. For some newcomers, learning to be honest is a process that takes time and many failures. Some of us have lied to ourselves and others about so many things for so long that we barely know what the truth is when we finally make it into the program.

> *Learning to be honest is a process for some of us.*

There is no reason for us, therefore, to expect instant honesty from a newcomer sponsee. Dishonesty is something that the two of us can be aware of as a problem and work on together. This approach isn't intended to provide an excuse for lying, but to allow progress (rather than to demand perfection) in this area. On the other hand, I do expect my sponsee to be honest about his drinking or drug use (or equivalent addiction or compulsion) and about the fundamentals of his program.

> *Help your sponsees work on being honest*
> *with themselves and with others.*

My sponsee calls too often. How do I handle that?

Set your boundaries. You have a right to your time. Discuss the situation and try to resolve it. If it's a matter of excessive dependency, address that issue. If your sponsee simply wants to talk with you more than you want to talk with him or her, discuss the problem openly and try to resolve the conflicting expectations by coming to a mutually acceptable compromise.

What do I do when my sponsee is seeing a therapist who says that the sponsee doesn't have to work the Steps because they are covering his or her basic problems in therapy?

First, a little background. Beginning in the summer of 1944, after nine years of sobriety, Bill Wilson sought treatment for depression from Harry Tiebout, M.D., a nonalcoholic psychiatrist. Dr. Tiebout was an early and enthusiastic supporter of AA, and the two men developed a "longstanding" friendship.[1] During this period, Bill Wilson relied on AA and its Twelve Steps to keep him sober. He relied on Dr. Tiebout to help him make progress on other issues in his life. Dr. Tiebout never presumed to treat Bill's alcoholism.

> *Some sponsees may try to use therapy*
> *as an excuse for not working the Steps.*

Coming between your sponsee and his or her therapist is a no-win situation. You do have the right, however, to point out to your sponsee that Twelve Step programs are the most effective treatment for certain addictions and compulsions, a statement that is confirmed by scientific research.

What your sponsee claims the therapist has said and what the therapist has actually said may be very different. Ask your sponsee if he or she is trying to use the therapist as an excuse to avoid the hard work of the Steps. If your sponsee continually refuses to work the Steps, consider resigning as sponsor. Since your primary responsibility as a sponsor is to help your sponsee work the Steps, you cannot work effectively with a sponsee who won't work them.

What if my sponsee is suicidal?

There is no easy answer to this difficult question. Each situation is different. If there is a clear and present danger, you may need to suggest that your sponsee call 911. Otherwise, we have a responsibility to see that our sponsee has told a member of his or her family (spouse, sibling, parent) about the suicidal feelings *or* that he or she has sought professional help. Beyond that, all you can do is be available on a reasonable basis and turn it over. The basic guideline is that you are not in charge of your sponsee's life, and even a decision as profoundly important as life or death is his or hers to make. It is not within your power to keep someone alive.

Suggest to suicidal sponsees
that they seek professional help.

You also have a responsibility to yourself in these cases. Should your sponsee commit suicide, you want to know that you have done everything you could reasonably have done to prevent it. In other words, in the tragic event that your sponsee follows through with the threat of suicide, you don't want to burden yourself with guilt because you did not urge him or her to get help. Ask yourself what reasonable behavior would be under the circumstances. Seek the advice of your sponsor. Do what you can. Turn over the results.

How do I know when I am "carrying" my sponsee?

We are carrying a sponsee when the sponsee has little commitment to Twelve Step recovery and is participating only because of our pressure. If the relationship is largely one-sided, and it feels as though your sponsee isn't bearing his or her fair share of the relationship, you may be carrying that sponsee. For example, you initiate the telephone calls, take the sponsee to meetings he or she won't attend otherwise, and make continuous suggestions that are ignored. One way to test for this condition is to avoid calling your sponsee for a while and see what happens. If your sponsee does not call you, you have probably been carrying him or her. One of AA's great sayings is, "We carry the message, not the alcoholic." Let the sponsee go.

We carry the message, not the sponsee.

What do I do with a sponsee who is obviously depressed?

There is not an easy answer to this question. A significant percentage of alcoholics and addicts are depressed when they get clean and sober (alcohol, after all, is a depressant). Some of us come out of that depression rather quickly in recovery while others do not. Some depressed members of the Fellowship need professional help. The difference between "being depressed" and the chronic, pathological condition of depression is not one that most program members are qualified to determine.

One effective technique that is often suggested for getting out of a depression is to make a gratitude list. Take out a pad of paper and write, "Things to be grateful for" at the top. Start with "I'm sober (clean, abstinent) today" and continue the list, writing down every single thing you can think of to be grateful for. By the time your arm is sore, you may have a different outlook on things.

When your sponsee is depressed, suggest
that he or she make a gratitude list.

What do I do if I think my sponsee is relapsing?

If the evidence is strong enough to make you suspicious, ask him or her about it. You must have some reason for suspecting it, so a discussion of that reason is in order. Rumors are not reliable, so it would have to be some action on your sponsee's part, some change in attitude or behavior, or some eyewitness account that made you suspicious. As a rule, you will find out soon enough. An alcoholic or addict finds it is very difficult to conceal his or her drinking or using from another alcoholic or addict. We know them too well.

What do I do if my sponsee slips?

Ask your sponsee if he or she has a desire to stop drinking, using, or engaging in compulsive behavior. If your sponsee wants to quit, get him or her to a Twelve Step meeting as soon as possible, and follow the guidelines in the answer to the following question.

If your sponsee does not want to get clean or sober or abstinent, or claims to want recovery but is unwilling to attend a Twelve Step meeting, there is nothing more you can do except be available should he or she decide otherwise. As the saying goes, Twelve Step recovery is not for those who *need* it, but for those who *want* it.

What if my sponsee slips and wants to get back in recovery?

Get him or her to a meeting as quickly as possible, preferably one where he or she can pick up a new desire chip. This symbol of starting over, admitting powerlessness, and asking for help can be powerful. Then

1. Welcome your sponsee back into the Fellowship.
2. Get your sponsee started immediately on the First Step.
3. Reestablish him or her on a newcomer's program of ninety meetings in ninety days, daily calls to check in, prayer and meditation, readings in the Big Book or equivalent, and so on.
4. Help your sponsee learn from the slip. What did he or she do or not do that contributed to the relapse? What should he or she do differently in the future to protect against another one?

When a sponsee slips,
get him or her to a meeting as quickly as possible.

What if my sponsee asks for money, a place to live, or to borrow my car?

Tell him or her that the answer is no. Sponsorship is a special relationship created to help your sponsee stay in recovery by helping him or her work the Twelve Step recovery program. If you try to make it into something other than that (a love relationship, a buddy relationship, a banking relationship, an employer relationship), it may destroy the usefulness of the sponsorship.

Friendships and families—not to mention sponsorships— have broken up over questions of money. One of the ground rules from the beginning should be to not lend money, furnish lodging, provide an automobile, or do similar favors for a sponsee. These services are not part of the purpose of sponsorship. Refuse any effort by your sponsee to abuse the relationship in this manner.

If you want to lend your sponsee money, you can certainly do so, but then ask him or her to find another sponsor.

Sponsorship is a special relationship created for a single purpose: to help sponsees recover by applying Twelve Step principles in all their affairs.

How much advice on matters outside the program should I give my sponsee?

Darn little. We are not in a position to advise our sponsees on their jobs, their spouses, their girlfriends, their boyfriends, or whether or not they should go back to college. What we can suggest is that they apply the Steps to these issues, especially the Third and Eleventh, and practice Twelve Step principles in all their affairs. One of AA's Twelve Promises is that AA members will intuitively know how to handle situations that used to baffle them. If our sponsees rely on the Steps and their Higher Power, the answers will take care of themselves.

What if my sponsee has a dual addiction?

When the sponsee is a newcomer, it makes sense for him or her to attend Twelve Step meetings for a secondary chemical addiction if he or she is comfortable doing so. Each Twelve Step program claims expertise only in its particular area. It makes no claim whatsoever to being able to help somebody with any other addiction. So the decision about going to other Twelve Step meetings is one that you and your sponsee should discuss.

A sponsee with a dual addiction may need to attend a second Twelve Step program to deal with that addiction.

My sponsee just wants to be my buddy. Is that okay?

No, it is not. Your role as a sponsor is more purposeful than that of a buddy. Our conversations with our sponsees should be semistructured in that we focus with them on how they are applying Twelve Step principles in their lives. Did they work on their character defects today? When they were wrong, did they promptly admit it? Have they sought through prayer and meditation to know the will of God as they understand God? Have they helped another alcoholic or addict? Did they go to a meeting? Have they been honest with themselves and others? These are the kinds of questions we ask as sponsors. They are not our only questions, of course, but they provide the framework for our conversations. They are not the kinds of issues that generally come up in buddy talk.

Sponsorship is a structured relationship with a specific agenda: helping the sponsee work the Twelve Steps and stay in recovery.

When should I suggest that my sponsee seek professional help?

The term "professional help" usually refers to a psychiatrist, psychologist, or other therapist who deals with emotional problems, and that is the way I have used it in this answer. I recommend to suicidal sponsees that they seek professional help immediately. In those cases where my sponsee's problems seem to be more than addiction or compulsion alone, where he is suffering terribly without relief despite his best efforts to work the Steps, I suggest that some form of counseling might be called for. The AA Big Book refers to "our psychologist" as one with whom to share our Fifth Step,[2] so there is precedence for it. Furthermore, Bill Wilson saw a psychiatrist for his depression,[3] and AA statements make it clear that the Fellowship has no quarrel with mental health professionals. In an address to the New York City Medical Society on Alcoholism, Bill Wilson said, "We know, too, that psychiatry can often release the big neurotic overhang from which many of us suffer after A.A. has sobered us up."[4]

The decision to seek professional help is your sponsee's. Only he or she can decide whether or not it is right. Many emotional problems do clear up after a period of recovery in a Twelve Step program. Others do not. The decision has to be made case by case.

Some sponsees need to seek professional help.

What if my sponsee hasn't called me in weeks?

It depends on how new your sponsee is to the program and to the relationship and whether or not you have called him or her. Several weeks is a long time not to have talked with a sponsee. A sponsee who hasn't initiated a call in a long time or hasn't returned your phone calls is probably in emotional trouble or no longer interested in your sponsorship. On the other hand, maybe he or she is on vacation. You will have to determine what's going on. Confront your sponsee, and try to resolve the problem.

PART III

Working the Steps

8

Introducing
the Steps

A sponsor's single most important responsibility to a sponsee is to help him or her work the Twelve Steps. To work a Step means to understand its principles and apply them to daily living. The term "work" is appropriate because the process involves a lot of effort. Chapters 8 through 20 provide an introduction to the Steps, including their history and themes, and describe a detailed program for working each of the Twelve Steps with your sponsees.

Purpose of the Steps

For members of Twelve Step Fellowships, the Steps serve a specific purpose. According to AA cofounder Bill Wilson, their author, the Twelve Steps "are a group of principles, spiritual in their nature, which, if practiced as a way of life, can expel the obsession to drink and enable the sufferer to become happily and usefully whole."[1] In other words, the Twelve Steps can keep us, as alcoholics, sober and happy. They serve a similar function for other Twelve Step Fellowships by relieving their members of addictive or compulsive behaviors and thoughts. Dr. Bob, AA's cofounder, said, "Our Twelve Steps, when simmered down . . . resolve themselves into the words 'love' and 'service.' "[2]

The Twelve Steps can keep us happy and in recovery.

The Twelve Steps are introduced in chapter 5 of the AA Big Book with these words, "Rarely have we seen a person fail who has thoroughly followed our path."[3] "Our path" is the Twelve Steps. They are the heart of recovery. To work the program is to work the Twelve Steps. To live the program is to live the Twelve Steps. AA's Promises are said to come true with working the Ninth Step. A spiritual awakening occurs by the Twelfth Step. The freedom and happiness of millions of alcoholics, Al-Anon members, drug addicts, compulsive gamblers, sex addicts, compulsive eaters, compulsive spenders, and others, are based on these twelve simple Steps.

History of the Steps

The first members of Alcoholics Anonymous relied on a word-of-mouth program to stay sober. As the Fellowship grew and spread to distant cities, the AA pioneers were afraid that their program would get seriously distorted in its constant retelling. They decided, therefore, to write down what they had learned in a book to be given to new members. The foreword to the first edition of the AA Big Book states, "We, of Alcoholics Anonymous, are more than one hundred men and women who have recovered from a seemingly hopeless state of mind and body. To show other alcoholics *precisely how we have recovered* is the main purpose of this book."[4]

Bill Wilson took on the task of writing the first part of the book. At chapter 5, he realized that he would "have to tell how our program for recovery from alcoholism really worked. The backbone of the book would have to be fitted in right here."[5] The "backbone of the book" was the Steps. Until then, AA's word-of-mouth program had been based on six Steps. These Steps are described by Bill Wilson in *Alcoholics Anonymous Comes of Age: A Brief History of A.A.,* as follows:

1. We admitted that we were licked, that we were powerless over alcohol.
2. We made a moral inventory of our defects or sins.
3. We confessed or shared our shortcomings with another person in confidence.
4. We made restitution to all those we had harmed by our drinking.
5. We tried to help other alcoholics, with no thought of reward in money or prestige.
6. We prayed to whatever God we thought there was for power to practice these precepts [principles].[6]

AA's recovery program began with six steps.

Later in *Alcoholics Anonymous Comes of Age,* Bill described the process by which he wrote the new Steps for chapter 5 of the Big Book:

> Finally I started to write. I set out to draft more than six steps; how many more I did not know. I relaxed and asked for guidance. With a speed that was astonishing, considering my jangling emotions, I completed the first draft. It took perhaps half an hour. The words kept right on coming. When I reached a stopping point, I numbered the new steps. They added up to twelve. Somehow this number seemed significant.[7]

The Twelve Steps were published in the AA Big Book in April 1939.

Chapter 5 of the AA Big Book
contains the Twelve Steps

For interpreting the meaning of the Twelve Steps, the Big Book and *Twelve Steps and Twelve Traditions* (the Twelve and Twelve) are the basic AA authorities. Because Bill Wilson wrote both books[8] as well as the Steps themselves, his other writings on the Steps are also authoritative. The Twelve and Twelve is an important addition to the AA Big Book because of its detailed treatment of the Steps. According to the foreword, the book "presents an explicit view of the principles by which A.A. members recover"[9] and "broadens and deepens the understanding of the Twelve Steps as first written"[10] in the Big Book. The Twelve and Twelve was published in April 1952.

> **Bill Wilson wrote the Twelve Steps and Twelve Traditions**
> **to broaden and deepen our understanding of the Steps.**

Why the Steps Are "Suggested"

The suggested nature of the Twelve Step program of recovery allows us as addicts or alcoholics to make our own decisions about working the Steps and about applying their principles in our lives. Responsibility for working a Twelve Step program rests squarely on our own shoulders. No one will force us to do anything. The lack of rules, regulations, and required Steps keeps us from a state of rebellion that would work against us. Bill Wilson writes in the Twelve and Twelve, "Alcoholics Anonymous does not demand that you believe anything. All of its Twelve Steps are but suggestions."[11]

> **By calling the Twelve Steps "suggested,"**
> **the Fellowship left the decision to work them entirely up to us.**

The fact is, however, that while the Twelve Steps are only *suggested*, they do make up the recovery program. And it is the Fellowship's *only* program. Working them is crucial, therefore, to the achievement and maintenance of sobriety. Perhaps the best way to summarize the suggested nature of the Twelve Steps is this: We don't have to work the Twelve Steps unless we want to stay in recovery.

> **Recovery is a daily choice we make.**

What It Means to "Work" a Step

It is not coincidental that the term "work" is used to describe the application of the Twelve Steps to our daily lives. Bill Wilson writes, "All of the Twelve Steps require sustained and personal exertion to conform to their principles. . . ."[12] While recovery itself may be by grace, the joy of recovery is earned by hard work. That work is defined by the Steps.

"Working a Step" or "taking a Step" consists of two phases: the first phase is gaining an understanding of what the Step means. It could be called "understanding the Step." This learning phase is undertaken in a formal way with a sponsor. It involves reading the AA Big Book or equivalent and other Conference-approved literature, talking with other group members, and carrying out whatever reading assignments a sponsor makes. The objective of this phase is to get our sponsee to understand the Step *as it relates to him or her* and to feel it *emotionally*. It is not enough merely to appreciate the meaning of the Step intellectually.

> *The first phase of working a Step*
> *is understanding what the Step means.*

The second phase of working a Step is a conscious effort to change our behavior in accordance with the principles of the Step. This phase could be called "applying the Step." In other words, it is the application of the principles of the Step to daily life. This phase of the Step involves attending meetings to hear how others apply the Steps, prayer and meditation, and daily, disciplined effort. It means asking ourselves, "How does this Step apply specifically to my life?" and "How do I change my behavior to live its principles?" It is not easy to change the ingrained habits, thought patterns, and perceptions of a lifetime. Yet that is exactly what the second phase of working the Steps is about.

> *The second phase of working a Step*
> *is to apply its principles to our daily lives.*

The Twelve Steps are designed to bring about a spiritual awakening. The Twelfth Step makes this purpose clear: "Having had a spiritual awakening as the result of these steps. . . ." It is the spiritual awakening that removes the compulsion and brings about our recovery. For the spiritual awakening to occur, the Twelve Steps should be worked in the prescribed order, one Step at a time, beginning with the First Step. Each Step flows logically from the one before it and builds upon its principles. Practically speaking, when we work a Step, we are working all the previous Steps as well. Therefore, we cannot skip Steps and effectively work a Twelve Step program.

> *The Twelve Steps make up a complete program.*
> *Each Step is supposed to be worked in order.*

Because the order of the Steps is not random, conventional Twelve Step wisdom suggests that when a sponsee is having difficulty working a Step, it is because he or she has not completed the prior Step. Many a sponsor has helped a sponsee break a logjam of inaction by suggesting that he or she return to the previous Step to work it more thoroughly.

> *Usually, when we are having trouble working a Step,*
> *it's because we haven't completed work on the previous one.*

Timing of the Steps

A newcomer is ready to begin the First Step as soon as he or she becomes your sponsee. Start him or her on Step One and provide a general introduction to the Steps along the lines of this chapter.

A new sponsee who is not a newcomer to the program should participate with you in a thorough review of his or her whole recovery program, including the Steps that he or she has worked. After such a review, some sponsees realize that they have not worked as many Steps as they had thought. In such cases, they return to the first un-worked Step.

> *Your new sponsees should review each of the Steps with you*
> *to be sure they have actually worked them.*

There is no prescribed timetable for taking each of the Steps. Since both the AA Big Book and the Twelve and Twelve are silent on the issue of timing (except between some individual Steps), the opinions expressed here are strictly my own. They are based on an analysis of Twelve Step literature and historical practices, interviews with other Twelve Step members, and my own experience.

In AA's earliest days when its recovery program consisted of only six steps, the steps were taken quickly, beginning with "the surrender." The surrender in its original form was an element of early Twelve Step work that was later abandoned. It is described in the following paragraph from *Dr. Bob and the Good Oldtimers: A Biography, with Recollections of Early A.A. in the Midwest.*

> The surrender was more than important; it was a must. Bob E., who came into A.A. in February 1937, recalled that after five or six days in the hospital, "when you had indicated that you were serious, they told you to get down on your knees by the bed and say a prayer to God admitting you were powerless over alcohol and your life was unmanageable. Furthermore, you had to state that you believed in a Higher Power who would return you to sanity. There you can see the beginning of the Twelve Steps," he said. "We called that the surrender. They [Dr. Bob and the original AA members] demanded it. You couldn't go to a meeting until you did it. If by accident you didn't make it in the hospital, you had to make it in the upstairs bedroom over [at the Oxford Group/AA meeting] at the Williams' house."[13]
>
> After the surrender, many of the steps—involving inventory, admission of character defects, and making restitution—were taken within a matter of days.[14]

> **Early AA practice was to take the Steps quickly.**

"Step Nine" in the Twelve and Twelve (written by Bill Wilson in 1952) gives us some additional insight into the timing of the Steps. Referring to the amends called for in Step Nine, Bill writes, "We may not want to say anything for several weeks, or longer. First we will wish to be reasonably certain that we are on the A.A. beam."[15]

The implication of this passage is that the Ninth Step could be taken "several weeks" into sobriety.

We know from AA history that it was the preference of Bill, Dr. Bob, and the AA pioneers to move new AA members rapidly through the Steps. The fundamental guideline, therefore, based on practice and tradition, seems to be for sponsees to work the Steps as quickly as possible while still being thorough. The Steps are, after all, the key to achieving and maintaining sobriety, so that approach makes sense. In the thirty-day inpatient treatment programs for chemical dependency that were prevalent in the 1980s, it was customary for the recovering alcoholic to have taken Steps One through Five by the time he or she had finished treatment.

Because the Steps are the key to a lasting and rewarding sobriety, they should be worked as quickly as possible while still being thorough.

The timing of the Steps will naturally vary from sponsee to sponsee. What is appropriate for one may not be appropriate for another. As sponsors, we must feel our way along with our sponsees on this matter; however, the general guideline is to maintain a firm but gentle pressure to keep working the Steps. The idea sometimes heard in meetings of taking "one Step a year" is not supported by Twelve Step literature or tradition.

Step Study

One of the characteristics of this book is its assumption that studying is an important part of Step work. By assigning sponsees specific passages to read and questions to answer, we can provide a structure for their efforts and actively involve them in Step study. Without readings from the basic text of our Fellowship and the Twelve and Twelve or equivalent, it is difficult for them to learn what the Steps mean, what is expected of them with each of the Steps, and how the Steps can make a difference in their lives. These are programs of action based on the Twelve Steps. Your sponsee needs the direction and guidance that you can provide to work the Steps successfully.

Readings from the AA Big Book or equivalent
increase a sponsee's understanding of the Steps.

Providing the study suggestions, reviewing the readings yourself, scheduling meetings, and answering your sponsee's questions take time and energy. There is no shortcut for us as sponsors, just as there is no shortcut for our sponsees. There is a Twelve Step saying that fits here: "You can't give away what you don't have." Sponsors who want to help their sponsees with the Steps have to know the Steps themselves. If we haven't worked the Steps, if we aren't growing in the Steps, if we aren't deepening our own understanding of the Steps, we're not in a position to help our sponsees. Teaching the Steps is a form of Twelve Step work through which we learn too.

When making study suggestions, it is helpful to remind sponsees of two things:

1. They don't have to do the readings if they don't want to. But if they don't want to, it is appropriate to discuss the reasons for their unwillingness and their lack of commitment to studying the Steps.
2. Sponsees will not be tested on the material, and they won't be graded on it. The reason for the readings and the questions is to help them understand what the Step means and to give them some information they can use in discussing the Step with you. The readings will also familiarize them with program literature and resources so they can find authoritative answers to their questions about the Steps.

As sponsors, we are not authorities on the Steps.
The AA Big Book and the Twelve and Twelve or equivalents
are the authoritative sources.

Formal Meetings with Sponsees

It has been my experience that sponsees require formal meetings devoted exclusively to Step work if they are to work the Steps satisfactorily. Step work cannot be accomplished just over the telephone, in brief encounters after meetings, or in other haphazard ways. The basic structure we can provide for working the Steps consists of suggested readings and questions followed by discussions with our sponsees. It is through these discussions based on the readings that we can teach our sponsees the meaning of the Steps.

One or two formal meetings may be all that are required for each Step. The first meeting is an introduction to the Step and is held after your sponsee has finished his or her suggested readings and study questions. In that meeting, I

- Read the Step.
- Remind my sponsee that what I have to say about the Step is strictly my own opinion.
- Reassure my sponsee that our discussion will not be a test on the readings.
- Explain in a general way what I think the Step means.
- Discuss the Step in terms of the suggested readings and questions. I base that discussion on the ideas contained in the following chapters on the Steps (chapters 9 to 20).
- Try to answer any questions he may have.

During formal meetings on the Steps,
have a copy of the basic text of the Fellowship
available for reference purposes.

After the first meeting on the Step, a lot of work can be accomplished over the telephone and after meetings as your sponsee goes through the process of understanding and applying the principles of the Step to his or her life.

The last formal meeting occurs when your sponsee "takes" the Step in your presence. The way in which the Step is taken differs for each Step. This final meeting helps create a rite of passage that brings a sense of completion to the Step and moves your sponsee on to the next Step.

A formal meeting that "completes" the Step
will help move your sponsee on to the next one.

Format of the Chapters on the Steps

Chapters 9 through 20 contain an organized program to assist you in the process of leading your sponsees through the Steps. These chapters can be used like lesson plans for teaching the meaning of the Steps and how they can be applied. Each chapter covers one Step completely.

Because there are so many different Twelve Step programs, I could not list the specific readings for each of them. Therefore, I have listed those readings that apply to members of Alcoholics Anonymous. If you are a member of another Twelve Step Fellowship, check your basic text and Twelve and Twelve equivalent and other appropriate Conference-approved literature for the specific pages to assign your sponsees to read. I have left space for you to write in the names of the references and the page numbers.

The wording of the Steps differ slightly in the various Twelve Step programs. Rather than try to reword the AA Steps at the beginning of each chapter to make them fit all of the different programs, I have chosen to quote them in their original form. For sponsors and sponsees in Fellowships other than AA, cross out and add the necessary words to adapt the Steps to your Fellowship.

All the Step chapters are divided into the same five sections to make it easier for you to follow the format and help your sponsee work the Step. You can use the chapter as a reference from the moment your sponsee begins work on the Step to the final meeting in which he or she formally takes it with you. The contents of

each Step chapter is shown below and is explained in the following paragraphs:

CHAPTER CONTENTS FOR EACH STEP

1. Timing of the Step
2. Step study
3. Understanding the Step
4. Applying the Step
5. Sponsor guidelines

1. *Timing of the Step:* How to tell when your sponsee is ready
   to work the Step or how soon a Step should follow the previous Step.
2. *Step study:* Suggested readings and questions for your sponsee
   to help him or her understand the Step. The questions are
   based on my personal experience, conversations with other
   program members, and on the assigned readings from AA's Big
   Book and Twelve and Twelve. Substitute the basic text and page
   numbers of your own Fellowship when making reading assignments and add whatever questions you think are appropriate.
3. *Understanding the Step:* An interpretation of the Step that you
   can use as a basis for discussing the Step with your sponsee.
   This portion of the chapter breaks the Step into its various
   parts, ideas, or phrases and answers the questions that were
   given with the readings. Since this interpretation is based on
   my own understanding of Twelve Step literature, on discussions with other program members, and on my own experience, you may not agree with it. Use what you do agree with
   and find useful. Ignore the rest. You may want to have your
   sponsee read this portion of the book in preparation for discussing the Step, but it isn't necessary.
4. *Applying the Step:* How your sponsee can apply the Step to
   daily life.
5. *Sponsor guidelines:* How to walk your sponsee through the Step.
   These guidelines include suggestions for structuring the final
   meeting in which your sponsee will formally take the Step.

Since each Step chapter follows exactly the same outline, you can use this book as a ready reference for

- Suggesting specific readings and questions for each Step.
- Discussing the meaning of the Step.
- Structuring the last meeting on the Step so that your sponsee has a sense of having "taken" the Step.

No two sponsees will work the Steps in the same way, just as no two sponsors will guide their sponsees through the Steps in the same way. These chapters propose a set of guidelines, suggestions, and recommendations. Certain suggestions will appeal to you more than others. Some recommendations will match your style of sponsoring and some will not. The Step chapters are detailed because they were written for those who are new to sponsoring as well as for those who like detailed suggestions. If you are an experienced sponsor or you prefer to "wing it," use those suggestions that you find useful and ignore the rest.

9

Working Step One

We admitted we were powerless over alcohol— that our lives had become unmanageable. [Twelve Step Fellowships other than AA or Al-Anon substitute words like "food," "our addiction," "spending," or "compulsive sexual behavior" for alcohol.]

Timing of Step One

A newcomer is ready to begin Step One as soon as he or she enters the program. Suggest that your newcomer sponsee start working the First Step as soon you become his or her sponsor.

Step Study

The following readings and questions are suggested for your sponsee as preparation for taking Step One. Answers to the questions can be found in the readings, in "Understanding the First Step" later in this chapter, and in your sponsee's personal experience.

Readings on the Step

1. Chapter 2 ("There Is a Solution") and chapter 3 ("More About Alcoholism") in the AA Big Book (pages 17–43).

2. "Step One" in the AA Twelve and Twelve (pages 21–24).
3. Other readings on the Step appropriate to your particular Twelve Step program: _____

_____

4. _____

_____

Questions about the Step

1. What does it mean to "admit" something?
2. Why do you think the Step says, "*We* admitted" rather than "*I* admitted?"
3. What does the term "powerless over alcohol" mean?
4. What does the term "our lives had become unmanageable" mean?

Activities for the Step

1. Make a list of specific examples of your powerlessness over alcohol (or narcotics, sex, food, or whatever the addictive substance or compulsive behavior of your Fellowship).
2. Make a list of specific examples of how your life has become unmanageable.

Understanding the First Step

The AA Big Book devotes two entire chapters to Step One. The First Step is so basic to recovery that the AA Twelve and Twelve says it is the only Step that we can practice with "absolute perfection."[1] Step One is an admission of the central problem we face as addicts: our powerlessness over an addictive substance or compulsive behavior and the unmanageable life that has resulted. Once we can admit our powerlessness, a door opens to the solution to our problem. As long as we deny our powerlessness, however, our problem cannot be solved.

In Step One, we admit our powerlessness.

Step One is the only Step that mentions the addictive substance, addiction, or object of our compulsion and our problem with it: powerlessness. Beginning with Step Two, the next eleven Steps describe a series of actions to solve that problem. It is significant that only one Step of the twelve deals with the problem, and that the other eleven Steps focus on its solution. AA and its sister Fellowships are about living in the solution—not in the problem.

Key concepts

THE MEANING OF POWERLESSNESS

"We alcoholics are men and women who have lost the ability to control our drinking," says the AA Big Book. "We know that no real alcoholic *ever* recovers control."[2] The First Step is about admitting defeat in our battle with alcohol or whatever our addiction or compulsion. But Step One is not merely an intellectual admission of powerlessness. It is an emotional acceptance of our powerlessness made at the gut level. It is surrender, and in the early days of AA, the Step was taken on one's knees. The AA Twelve and Twelve refers to this acceptance of powerlessness and unmanageability as an experience of "utter defeat," "bankruptcy," "hopelessness," and "hitting bottom." As the AA Big Book says, "We learned that we had to fully concede [admit] to our innermost selves that we were alcoholics. This is the first step in recovery."[3]

Why must the experience of the First Step be so painful, so devastating, so complete? Because, as the AA Twelve and Twelve tells us,

> . . . Few people will sincerely try to practice the A.A. program unless they have hit bottom. . . . Who wishes to be rigorously honest and tolerant? Who wants to confess his faults to another and make restitution for harm done? Who cares anything about a Higher Power, let alone meditation and prayer? Who wants to sacrifice time and energy in trying to carry A.A.'s message to the

next sufferer? No, the average alcoholic, self-centered in the extreme, doesn't care for this prospect—unless he has to do these things in order to stay alive himself.[4]

> *It is the desperation we feel at "hitting bottom"*
> *that motivates us to do the hard work of the program.*

As the AA Big Book says, "All of us felt at times that we were regaining control, but such intervals—usually brief—were inevitably followed by still less control, which led in time to pitiful and incomprehensible demoralization."[5] Early AA members used to recommend to new members who were still in doubt about their alcoholism to go out and try some "controlled drinking."[6] For example, have exactly two drinks a day for one month and see whether or not you can always stop after the second drink. A nonalcoholic can.

> *Controlled drinking*
> *is not possible for an alcoholic.*

Some examples of powerlessness are intending to have only one drink before an important meeting but having too many instead. Promising yourself not to drink at a reception, then deciding to just have one. Swearing that you won't use or overeat for a week, then doing it before the time is up. The basic texts of various Twelve Step Fellowships list numerous techniques that addicts have used to try to control their addictions or compulsions. Ask your sponsee if he or she has ever tried any of them.

THE MEANING OF UNMANAGEABILITY

When we deny our powerlessness over alcohol or whatever our addiction or compulsion, our lives become unmanageable. In Step One, we come to terms with that unmanageability. Our lives may be unmanageable in a few areas or in many areas. They may be slightly unmanageable in some areas and totally unmanageable in others. But they will be unmanageable. Unmanageability caused by addiction takes many forms. It can include physical, spiritual, and mental problems; financial and legal problems; family and social problems. The problems may have been obvious to others or known only to us, but they were there in one form or another.

The longer we are in recovery, the more we realize
how unmanageable our lives had become.

By accepting our powerlessness and unmanageability, we are accepting that we cannot recover alone. We will need help. That help, the AA Big Book tells us in the Second Step, will come from a Power greater than ourselves. So Step One lays the basis of our willingness to open ourselves to a Power greater than ourselves and to recovery.

"WE ADMITTED"

Use of the plural pronoun in the First Step emphasizes that we are not alone and that we do not work our recovery program alone. Twelve Step programs are "we" programs. "*I* get drunk; *we* stay sober" is an old AA saying. The "we" includes us, other program members, and our Higher Power. The first word of the First Step makes that point clear.

Twelve Step Fellowships are "we" programs.

WHAT THE FIRST STEP ACCOMPLISHES

Step One forces us to look at our addiction. In doing so, it addresses a unique symptom of our disease: denial. Addiction is the only disease in which the victim of the disease, as a symptom of the disease, does not believe that he or she has it despite conclusive evidence to the contrary. As the AA Big Book tells us, "The idea that somehow, someday he will control and enjoy his drinking is the great obsession of every abnormal drinker. The persistence of this illusion is astonishing. Many pursue it into the gates of insanity or death." The same denial often applies to other compulsions and addictions as well.

By bringing us to a state of powerlessness and surrender, the First Step does the following:

- Helps us break through our denial and accept the reality of our addiction. Without this acceptance, it is difficult for us to work the other Steps and to stay in recovery.
- Helps us to become willing to make the changes in our attitudes and behavior that recovery will require.
- Makes us teachable so that we can learn from the Steps, program literature, and our fellow program members who have maintained their recovery.
- Opens us to the need for a Power greater than ourselves to help us overcome our addiction.
- Begins the difficult process of ego-deflation in which we exchange our grandiosity, narcissism, and self-centeredness for maturity and humility.

> *Our surrender in the First Step*
> *makes us teachable and willing.*

Applying the Step

Some newcomers are so desperate and confused when they enter AA that they are relieved to discover that their alcoholism is a disease. Everything suddenly makes sense to them. Almost immediately, they accept their powerlessness and unmanageability and so take Step One. Many newcomers to other Twelve Step programs respond similarly.

Other newcomers are deep in denial and are very resistant to the idea of being alcoholic or otherwise addicted. These newcomers may face a struggle in working this Step. Their struggle is between the reality of powerlessness and unmanageability, on the one hand, and their denial on the other. For them, the First Step is a process of acceptance that takes time. Each sponsee will be different.

Sponsor Guidelines for Working Step One

Suggest that your sponsee do the readings and answer the questions listed under "Step Study." When your sponsee has completed this work, ask him or her to make an appointment with you to discuss the Step.

First meeting on Step One

Based on the suggested readings, "Understanding the First Step" in this chapter, and your own knowledge and experience, discuss Step One with your sponsee. You may want to use the study questions or "Understanding the First Step" as a discussion guide.

The objectives of working with a sponsee on Step One are to get him or her to

1. Accept his or her powerlessness over alcohol or another addictive substance or compulsive behavior, as the central problem to be solved.
2. Feel at the deepest, most painful level possible the sense of hopelessness and defeat that comes from this powerlessness, from having been beaten day after day by a more powerful foe. Without help, it is too much for us.
3. Feel at the deepest, most painful level possible how unmanageable his or her life has become as the result of the addiction.
4. Understand the meaning and the danger of denial and the necessity of overcoming it.
5. Accept that all his or her efforts at staying abstinent alone have failed.

One of the most effective ways to break through denial and bring about acceptance of powerlessness and unmanageability is to have your sponsee recount specific examples of powerlessness and unmanageability. How has your sponsee proven again and again that he or she is powerless over alcohol, drugs, or compulsions and that his or her life has become unmanageable?

*Specific examples of powerlessness and unmanageability
help us break through denial.*

Later discussions

If your sponsee is wrestling with this Step

· Have him or her return repeatedly to examples of the power-lessness and unmanageability that have made his or her life so desperate and unhappy.
· Suggest that your sponsee attend as many *speaker* meetings as possible to increase identification with other addicted or compulsive individuals.
· Suggest that he or she pray daily for the willingness to work this Step. (If your sponsee is an atheist or agnostic, suggest that he or she try it anyway, praying "to whom it may concern.")

Taking Step One

In this last meeting on the First Step, ask your sponsee to

· Explain his or her understanding of the phrases "powerless over _____" and "our lives had become unmanageable."
· Provide examples that demonstrate these conditions in his or her life.

Your sponsees have taken Step One when they can *feel* their powerlessness over their addiction and can acknowledge *emotionally* that their lives have become unmanageable. They should express a sense of fear and desperation. They ought to be having the kind of response to this Step that says, "But what am I going to do now?" There should be evidence of their having hit bottom, of defeat and surrender. If not, they haven't taken the Step and more work is required.

10

Working
Step Two

*Came to believe that a Power greater than ourselves
could restore us to sanity.*

Timing of Step Two

Your sponsee is ready to begin the Second Step as soon as he or
she has worked Step One.

Step Study

The following readings and questions are suggested for your sponsee as preparation for taking Step Two. Answers to the questions
can be found in the readings, in "Understanding the Second Step"
later in this chapter, and in your sponsee's personal experience.

Readings on the Step

1. The pages in the AA Big Book that cover Step Two (pages
   44–57).
2. "Step Two" in the AA Twelve and Twelve (pages 25–33).

3. Other readings on the Step appropriate to your particular Twelve Step program: _____

_____

4. _____

_____

Questions about the Step

1. What does the phrase "Power greater than ourselves" mean?
2. As used in this Step, what does the term "sanity" mean?
3. Why does the Step say that a Power greater than ourselves *could* restore us to sanity rather than *would* restore us to sanity?

"A Power greater than ourselves" and "restoration to sanity"
are key concepts of Step Two.

Understanding the Second Step

The Second Step is about hope, a Higher Power, and dealing with reality. It follows logically from the First. In Step One, we admitted our powerlessness over our addiction and the unmanageability of our lives. We surrendered and gave up. With that sense of surrender came feelings of fear, anger, and, finally, hopelessness. If we were powerless over our problem, how could we ever solve it?

"Lack of power, that was our dilemma."[1]

In Step Two, we are given the solution. Our situation is *not* hopeless. Far from it. There is hope, but that hope lies outside ourselves. As the AA Big Book says, "We had to find a power by which we could live, and it had to be a *Power greater than ourselves.* . . . But where and how were we to find this Power?"[2] In Step Two, we begin that search—an undertaking that will lead us through the remainder of the Twelve Steps.

In the Second Step,
we discover that our situation is not hopeless.

Working Step Two is a process. The first three words say as much: "Came to believe." Sometimes the Step is described in terms of those words. It is said that first we "came" physically to AA or another Twelve Step program. Then we "came to" out of our alcoholic, drug-induced, or compulsive fog. Finally we "came to believe" that a Power greater than ourselves could restore us to sanity.

In our Twelve Step Fellowships,
we came; we came to; we came to believe.

Key concepts

A POWER GREATER THAN OURSELVES

The blessings or the baggage of our religious experiences come into play with the Second Step. For some newcomers to Twelve Step programs, this Step raises an issue that is a problem for them: God. They jump to the conclusion that they are in a religious group bent on converting them. But Step Two asks us only to believe in a Power greater than *ourselves*. That's all. That Power may be God as described by a specific church, synagogue, or temple or it may be something else. It may even not be God at all as God is traditionally defined. The Twelve and Twelve suggests that "you can, if you wish, make A.A. itself your 'higher power.' Here's a very large group of people who have solved their alcohol problem. In this respect they are certainly a power greater than you, who have not even come close to a solution. Surely you can have faith in them. Even this minimum of faith will be enough."[3] What is true of AA in this regard is true of the other Fellowships as well.

The AA Big Book says, "We needed to ask ourselves but one short question, 'Do I now believe, or am I even willing to believe, that there is a Power greater than myself?'" As soon as a person can answer, "Yes, I do," we "emphatically assure" that person that he or she is on the way.[4]

All that is necessary is a **willingness**
to believe in a Power greater than ourselves.

While the Step allows us to conceive of a Power greater than ourselves as anything we want, the AA Big Book and the Twelve and Twelve call that Power "God." Even so, the Big Book reminds us, "Much to our relief, we discovered we did not need to consider another's conception of God. Our own conception, however inadequate, was sufficient to make the approach and to effect a contact with Him."[5] Our experience has been that the exact concept of the Power does not matter at the Second Step, only that some concept exists.

"To be doomed to an alcoholic death or to live on a spiritual basis are not always easy alternatives to face," suggests the AA Big Book.[6] And they are not. The Second Step continues the humbling process begun in the First Step. It is sometimes said in Twelve Step programs that all we need to know about God is *that we are not God.* This Step introduces the idea that we are not God—that there *is* a Power greater than ourselves. It is a humbling thought. And that is its purpose.

*What we need to know about God
is that there is one and we are not it.*

SANITY: WHAT IS IT?

The Second Step suggests that our behavior as alcoholics, addicts, or compulsive eaters, gamblers, or spenders has been more than just unmanageable—it has been insane. One definition of insanity that is often used in Twelve Step programs is this one: insanity is doing the same thing over and over, but expecting different results. By that definition, as alcoholics for example, we exhibited insane behavior whenever we took the first drink (expecting not to get drunk), drove while intoxicated again after the first DWI (expecting not to get stopped), drank just before that "big meeting" (expecting not to mess it up), and so forth. This definition of insanity is sound, but it describes a symptom rather than the cause.

When we were in our addiction,
our lives were more than unmanageable. They were insane.

Why would we continue to repeat the same behavior while expecting different results? Because as active alcoholics, addicts, or compulsive people, we often preferred fantasy to reality. The fantasy world to which we so often retreated was a form of insanity. For example, the idea that we could have just one drink, one hit of crack, or one snack was total fantasy. It was, strictly speaking, insane. Each of us has our own version of insanity, of the unreal beliefs that worked against us in our drinking, using, or compulsive days. The restoration to sanity that the Second Step describes is about getting out of our fantasies and learning to live in reality. It means exchanging the old beliefs we hold that aren't true for new ones that are.

Sanity means living in reality.
It is accepting life on life's terms.

Living in a fantasy world is a lonely business. We may have everything we want in fantasy, but we are alone there. It can't be any other way, because no one can come into our fantasy world for long. We may, in fantasy, be heroes or heroines, rich or accomplished, perfect or honored. But we will always be alone. The only place where we can interact with others is on the playing field of reality. The way out of our loneliness is to get out of our fantasy and into reality. A deep, rich sense of being alive comes only with reality, with that restoration to sanity.

Addiction has been described as the disease of loneliness.
The Fellowships give us a way out.

WHO ARRANGES THE RESTORATION TO SANITY?

It is a Power greater than ourselves that arranges the restoration to sanity. *We* do not arrange the restoration. Neither does a spouse, a new house, a nicer apartment, the right car, or a better-paying job. None of these things has the power to restore us to

sanity. But the Higher Power does. Recovery is based on acceptance of that spiritual fact. God as we understand God, working
with us and through us, can restore us to sanity. Before we can do
our part, however, we have to ally ourselves with that Power. We
begin that process in the Second Step.

> ### It is our Higher Power
> ### who restores us to sanity.

There is no authoritative record as to why Bill Wilson used the
word "could" rather than "would" with the phrase "restore us to
sanity." One possibility is that use of the word "could" indicates
that a restoration to sanity is not automatic. The Step does not say
that the Power *will* restore us to sanity, only that the Power *could*.
Whether or not the restoration occurs is up to us as well as to the
Higher Power. In other words, while faith is important, so is work.
The restoration is not going to happen by magic. We have to do
our part by diligently working the Twelve Steps.

THE BEAUTY OF THE STEP

The beauty of the Second Step is that the restoration to sanity
which the Step asks us to believe is possible has already begun.
Sanity is living life on life's terms: it is accepting reality. As recovering people, the great reality for us is that we are not able to
drink alcohol, use drugs, or engage in compulsive behavior. By
admitting our powerlessness in the First Step, we have given up
the insane idea that we can drink, use, eat, or gamble like non-
addicts. Our restoration to sanity has already begun.

Another reality for us is that addiction is a spiritual disease
which requires a spiritual awakening. That awakening, too, is
already under way. By surrendering in the First Step and accepting that a Power greater than ourselves could restore us to sanity
in the Second, we have already begun the journey that will lead us
to that spiritual awakening. And to a restoration to sanity.

By the Second Step,
our restoration to sanity has already begun.

Applying Step Two

The immediate application of Step Two is to prepare us for Step Three by opening our minds to the possibility of a Power greater than ourselves. Without that open-mindedness, Step Three will prove too much for us.

The Second Step also gives us hope to counteract the feeling of powerlessness and fear we experienced at the end of the First Step. That same sense of hope from the Second Step can be utilized whenever we need it in recovery. This Step reminds us that a Power greater than ourselves can restore us to a new level of sanity. When our character defects seem overwhelming or life appears too difficult and our humanly powers inadequate for what has to be done, we can return to the Second Step for the reassurance that a Power greater than ourselves can help us.

Step Two can be used throughout our lives
whenever we need hope.

Sponsor Guidelines for Working Step Two

Suggest that your sponsee do the readings and answer the questions listed under "Step Study." When your sponsee has completed this work, ask him or her to make an appointment with you to discuss the Step.

First meeting on Step Two

Based on the suggested readings, "Understanding the Second Step" in this chapter, and your own knowledge and experience, discuss Step Two with your sponsee. You may want to use the study questions or "Understanding the Second Step" as a discussion guide.

Later discussions

For some sponsees, working Step Two is a difficult process that takes a long time and considerable effort, especially if their past experience with religion has been negative. If your sponsee is having difficulty with the Step, suggest that he or she

- Pray for willingness to work this Step (if your sponsee is willing to pray).
- Reread the assigned pages from the AA Big Book or equivalent and the Twelve and Twelve or whatever other reading assignments you may have given.
- Return to Step One. Does he or she really accept powerlessness over the addiction or compulsion and the unmanageability of his or her life?
- Try to identify the stumbling blocks.
- Talk with other group members about how they worked this Step.

Taking Step Two

According to the AA Big Book, we have taken Step Two when our "adventures before and after" sobriety have convinced us of the following three "pertinent ideas": [7]

A. That we were alcoholic and could not manage our own lives.
B. That no human power could have relieved our alcoholism.
C. That God could and would if He were sought.

In other words, we have to have taken the First Step by admitting our powerlessness over alcohol or whatever our addiction or compulsion is and to the unmanageability of our lives. Then we have to be able to answer yes to the following question: "Do you believe that a Power greater than yourself can relieve your addiction and restore you to sanity?"

When a sponsee can do both, he or she has formally taken Step Two. When the Fellowship is other than AA, the same principles still apply.

11

Working
Step Three

*Made a decision to turn our will and our lives
over to the care of God* as we understood Him.

Timing of Step Three

A sponsee is ready for Step Three as soon as he or she has completed Step Two. Sponsees have taken Step Two when they have admitted their powerlessness over their addictive substance or compulsion; have accepted the unmanageability of their lives; and have come to believe that a Power greater than themselves can relieve their addiction and restore them to sanity.[1]

Step Study

The following readings and questions are suggested for your sponsee as preparation for taking Step Three. Answers to the questions can be found in the readings, in "Understanding the Third Step" later in this chapter, and in your sponsee's personal experience.

Readings on the Step

1. Those pages in the AA Big Book that cover Step Three (pages 60–64).

2. "Step Three" in the AA Twelve and Twelve (pages 34–41).

3. Other readings on the Step appropriate to your particular Twelve Step program: _____

_____

4. _____

_____

Questions about the Step

1. What does the phrase "God as we understood [God]" mean?
2. What is your concept of God (or Higher Power)?
3. What does it mean to turn "our will and our lives over to the care of God"?
4. What is the difference between a life run on self-will and a life that follows God's will, however you understand God?
5. How well has self-will served you to this point?
6. What is a recent example in your life of exercising self-will rather than following what you believe might be God's will?
7. How can you know God's will?
8. What reservations, if any, do you have about turning your will and your life over to the care of God as you understand God?
9. What does it mean to "make a decision"?

Understanding the Third Step

With the First Step, we accepted the fundamental problem we face as alcoholics or addicts: our powerlessness over alcohol, our addiction, or compulsion and the unmanageability of our lives. In the Second Step, we found the nature of the solution: a Power greater than ourselves who could restore us to sanity. In the Third Step, we discover how to make use of that solution by turning our will and our lives over to the care of that Power.

> **Step Three has been summarized us:**
> **I can't, God can, I think I'll let God.**

According to the AA Twelve and Twelve, ". . . the effectiveness of the whole A.A. program will rest upon how well and earnestly we have tried to come to a 'decision to turn our will and our lives over to the care of God as we understood Him.'"[2] And ". . . other Steps of the A.A. program can be practiced with success only when Step Three is given a determined and persistent trial."[3] These principles apply to other Twelve Step Fellowships as well.

Key concepts

GOD AS WE UNDERSTOOD GOD

Until we considered the meaning of a Power greater than ourselves in the Second Step, many of us had not thought about God in years except, perhaps, to ask for help in the worst of our scrapes. Others of us have thought about God, but attributed to God characteristics that were based on images we had developed as children and never changed. Still others of us mouthed the words of our religious faith without giving much thought to whether or not we believed them. Few of us had examined what our concept of God really was in the deepest recesses of our minds and spirits. That is what the Third Step asks us to do.

In the Third Step,
we examine our concept of God.

How do we imagine God to be? Do we see God as loving or punishing, as involved in our affairs or unconcerned about them, as forgiving or attacking? Do we see God as a parent or a friend? Do we see God as "Him," as "Her," or as "It"? Do we believe in God at all? The Twelve Steps and the Twelve Step Fellowships do not attempt to define God for us. "When, therefore, we speak to you of God, we mean your own conception of God,"[4] says the AA Big Book. God as we understood God is exactly that: the God of our understanding, even if it is no God at all. Whatever concept we ultimately choose is up to us as Twelve Step members. But everyone has some concept of God or of no-God that affects his or her life. This Step merely asks us to examine that concept and to work with it. And, if we find it necessary and desirable, to change it.

> *Each Twelve Step member*
> *chooses his or her own concept of God.*
> *Or of no-God.*

SELF-WILL

Step Three raises the issue of self-will and the extent to which it runs our lives. "Selfishness—self-centeredness! That, we think is the root of our troubles. Driven by a hundred forms of fear, self-delusion, self-seeking, and self-pity, we step on the toes of our fellows and they retaliate,"[5] says the AA Big Book. "So our troubles, we think, are basically of our own making. They arise out of ourselves, and the alcoholic is an extreme example of self-will run riot, though he usually doesn't think so."[6] The AA Twelve and Twelve reminds us that "each of us has had his own near-fatal encounter with the juggernaut of self-will, and has suffered enough under its weight to be willing to look for something better."[7]

> *Self-centeredness is the root of our troubles.*

What is that "something better"? The AA Big Book tells us: "This is the how and why of it. First of all, we had to quit playing God. It didn't work."[8] We could no longer insist on having our own way, on trying to control other people, on believing that we always know what's best for ourselves, the world, and everyone else. We had to develop humility. In order to do that, we had to be convinced "that any life run on self-will can hardly be a success."[9]

The self-centeredness of our drinking, using, or compulsive days brought us little real or lasting pleasure. The rich meaning that we hoped to find in life continued to escape us. Even when we thought we knew best, we were often proven wrong. Trying to have it our way hadn't worked as the years of unmanageability showed.

TURNING OVER OUR WILL AND OUR LIVES

Step Three continues the process of ego-deflation begun in Steps One and Two by introducing the idea that our human will must be subordinated to a greater will, to the will of God as we understand God. This act is humility at its most powerful: putting the Divine agenda before our own. It is the great antidote to grandiosity, to self-will run riot. Humility is not the same as humiliation, although it often feels like humiliation to our inflated egos.

Humility is not the same as humiliation.

Humility means appreciating our proper role in the world. It means understanding that while we make decisions about the *actions* of our lives, we do not make decisions about the *results* of those actions. The results belong to God to determine. We take the action and leave the results to God. Once our grandiosity lessens and we have a more realistic vision of our role in the world, we often feel great relief. The burden of having "to run the world" has been lifted.

What would it mean to turn our will and our lives over to the care of God? How are we even to know God's will for us? Such questions are at the heart of this Step. They are not questions that are casually asked or easily answered. But their answers form the basis of a meaningful life and a solid recovery and should not be ignored. Part of the fear and difficulty associated with this Step may relate to the necessity of wrestling with these issues. Few of us approach this Step without the nagging thought that if we turned our will and our lives over to the care of God (as we understand God), we would be called upon to do things that we do not want to do. Perhaps we view God's will as more difficult than our own, forgetting how little peace and satisfaction our self-will has brought us. Perhaps we simply don't want anyone else — God included — telling us what to do.

Humility is putting God's will before our own.

MAKING A DECISION

Step Three speaks of a *decision* to turn our will and our lives over to the care of God. It does not say that we turned our will and our lives over to God, only that we made a decision to do so. The inclusion of the word "decision" has been interpreted by some as an acknowledgment that we can turn our will and lives over to God only imperfectly and irregularly. As worded, the Step suggests that we are continually remaking the decision. In fact, for most of us that has proven to be the case. A Twelve Step expression that speaks to this pattern of behavior is, "I keep turning it over and taking it back."

> ***Step Three asks us to make a decision.***

OUR WILL AND OUR LIVES

There has been some speculation about the Step's use of the word "lives" instead of "life." Whatever the reason may be, a useful interpretation is that the plural reminds us to turn over *all* the "lives" in which our will manifests itself. For example, it is not enough to turn over to the care of God only our life as a Twelve Step member. We also turn over our lives as parents, spouses, friends, business people—*all our lives.*

KNOWING GOD'S WILL

Many of us who approach this Step are concerned about the challenge of knowing God's will for us. In order to turn our will over to the care of God, we have to know what that will is. How can we? The answer is not easy beyond a basic belief that continued recovery is part of it.

Any effort to know God's will is aided by being *open* to it. The more open we are to learning God's will for us, the more likely we are to discover it. When we allow self-will to run riot and insist on having our own way, it is difficult to determine God's will. We are especially resistant when we are certain about what *we* want. It is helpful to remember that we do not always know what is best for us since we cannot see the future. In fact, many of us in Twelve Step programs have discovered that some of the things we had wanted would have been bad for us had we received them.

> **To know God's will for us,**
> **we must first be open to it.**

Some of the things that we had dreaded, on the other hand, turned out to be good for us. Therefore, we try to be open to things that we don't think we want but that we might need. We keep in mind the saying, "God gives us what we need, not necessarily what we want." And, "God never gives us more than we can handle."

We have found many ways to try to learn the will of God in our Twelve Step programs. For example, through

1. *Regular prayer and meditation* in which we seek God's will for us (through prayer) and try to listen to what that will might be (through meditation).

> **Using prayer and meditation**
> **is one way to discover God's will.**

2. *Intuition.* One of AA's Twelve Promises is that "we will intuitively know how to handle situations that used to baffle us." In recovery, we learn to trust our intuitive sense about what to do in a challenging situation. When we have to make a difficult decision, we often write down the advantages and disadvantages of a course of action and discuss them with our sponsor. Then we ask our Higher Power to guide us and try to get an intuitive sense of what to do.

3. *Friends.* Many times, a friend has appeared at a crucial moment to say something to us that has given us the needed insight or push to follow some plan of action that later worked out well.

4. *Readings.* A chance opening of the basic text of our Fellowship, a favorite passage from an inspirational book, a program saying, or a phrase from the past has often provided

the unexpected but insightful guidance we needed in making a decision.

5. *Steps.* When we are unsure about what to do, we turn to the Steps. They often contain the answer to the dilemma we face.

We believe that God's will for us
always includes recovery.

Through these and other ways that we discovered, those of us in Twelve Step recovery have sought to learn the will of God. The process is often uncertain, but we believe that it works when we want it to work. That has been our experience, anyway.

Applying Step Three

The Third Step is applied daily in recovery. Sometimes hourly. Even minute by minute. The decision to turn our will and our lives over to the care of God is one that most of us make and remake during the course of a day. It seems that we make the decision *not* to turn over our will and our lives about as often as we make the decision to do it. The ego is not easily deflated, and we insist on the illusion of control.

It seems that we are as often
"taking it back" as "turning it over."

The AA Twelve and Twelve talks about this condition when it refers metaphorically to the key of willingness as unlocking the door to Step Three and to faith. "Once we have placed the key of willingness in the lock and have the door ever so slightly open, we find that we can always open it some more. Though self-will may slam it shut again, as it frequently does, it will always respond the moment we again pick up the key of willingness."10

The phrase "turn it over" is sometimes used to refer to the Third Step. The expression means to turn the results of whatever we are concerned about over to the care of God. The Step can be misinterpreted to mean that all we have to do in life is "turn it over." That is not what the Step means. Nothing in the Step relieves us of our responsibility to take action. What we turn over are the *results* of our actions, *not* the actions themselves. In accordance with this Step, however, we do try to bring those actions into line with what we believe to be God's will for us.

The AA Twelve and Twelve ties the Third Step to the Serenity Prayer. In that prayer, we ask God for the serenity to accept the things we cannot change. Perhaps the hardest thing about turning our will over to the care of God is accepting that we may not get what we want. The results may not please our shortsighted view of things. So we need acceptance. The Twelve and Twelve suggests one way to find it, "In all times of emotional disturbance or indecision, we can pause, ask for quiet, and in the stillness simply say: 'God grant me the serenity to accept the things I cannot change, courage to change the things I can, and the wisdom to know the difference. Thy will, not mine, be done.'"[11]

*The Serenity Prayer helps us stay centered
when things don't go our way.*

Sponsor Guidelines for Working Step Three

Suggest that your sponsee do the readings and answer the questions listed under "Step Study." When your sponsee has completed this work, ask him or her to make an appointment with you to discuss the Step.

First meeting on Step Three

Based on the suggested readings, "Understanding the Third Step" in this chapter, and your own knowledge and experience, discuss Step Three with your sponsee. You may want to use the study questions or "Understanding the Third Step" as a discussion guide.

Later discussions

As your sponsee struggles with this Step, return to the basic question: Why is your sponsee having trouble turning over his or her will and life? Is it because of a negative concept of God? Does he or she not trust God? Does he or she have a child's view of God that needs to be updated? Try to help your sponsee identify his or her problem with this Step.

In addition, suggest that your sponsee

· Pray about the Step, asking for guidance, courage, and willingness daily.
· Reread the applicable pages in the basic text of your Fellowship and the other literature that has been assigned.
· Keep a list of examples of self-will and how they are hurting him or her.
· Keep track of the times he or she tries to follow God's will and what it feels like.
· Return to Step Two.
· Talk with other program members about how they worked the Step.

Taking Step Three

Since the AA Big Book suggests that it is "very desirable to take this spiritual step with an understanding person," it is important for your sponsee to formally take it with you.

In this last meeting, ask your sponsee to tell you what Step Three means to him or her and how he or she intends to apply it. In this process, you may want to review each of the questions that were assigned in the homework.

The most important question is whether or not your sponsee has made a decision to turn his or her will over to the care of God. If he or she has, your sponsee has taken the Step.

Remind your sponsee that Step Three is not worked once and for all, however; it is worked daily. We may turn our will and our lives over to the care of God and take them back many times in a day. Spiritual progress, not perfection, is our goal.

Step Three is worked throughout our lives.

To conclude the Step, the AA Big Book suggests that the idea contained in the Third Step prayer be expressed, "voicing it without reservation." The wording itself is optional. Ask your sponsee to repeat in your presence the Third Step Prayer or his or her version expressing its central idea.

The Third Step prayer is found on page 63 of the AA Big Book. It reads, "God, I offer myself to Thee—to build with me and to do with me as Thou wilt. Relieve me of the bondage of self, that I may better do Thy will. Take away my difficulties, that victory over them may bear witness to those I would help of Thy Power, Thy Love, and Thy Way of Life. May I do Thy will always!"[12] Although this prayer comes from the AA Big Book, it applies equally well to other Twelve Step programs.

When your sponsee has finished the prayer, he or she has taken Step Three.

Some Twelve Step members
include the Third Step Prayer
in their daily meditation.

12

Working
Step Four

*Made a searching and fearless
moral inventory of ourselves.*

Timing of Step Four

The Third Step is to be followed "at once" by Step Four, according
to the AA Big Book. Your sponsee is therefore ready to work on
the Fourth Step as soon as he or she has taken Step Three.

Step Study

The following readings and questions are suggested for your
sponsee as preparation for taking Step Four. Answers to the
questions can be found in the readings, in "Understanding the
Fourth Step" later in this chapter, and in your sponsee's personal
experience.

Step Four has two phases. The first phase is Step study in
which your sponsee completes the Step study readings, answers
the study questions, and discusses the Step with you until he or
she understands the meaning of the Step and what it requires. The
second phase is writing the Fourth Step inventory.

Readings on the Step

1. Those pages in the AA Big Book that cover Step Four (pages 63–71).
2. "Step Four" in the AA Twelve and Twelve (pages 42–54).
3. Other readings on the Step appropriate to your particular Twelve Step program: _____

_____

4. _____

_____

Questions about the Step

1. What is an inventory and what is its purpose?
2. What does the term "searching and fearless" mean?
3. Why is it a "moral" inventory that we are asked to do?
4. Why does the AA Big Book suggest that the inventory be *written?*
5. What format, strategy, or outline do you intend to use in writing your Fourth Step inventory?
6. What is a resentment? Why are resentments "the number one offender"?

Activities for the Step

1. Pray daily to your Higher Power for the courage and willingness to work this Step. The wording of the prayer should be your own, but it might be on the order of: "God, give me the strength and the courage to see what I need to see about myself, remember what I need to remember, and do what I need to do to complete my Fourth Step inventory."
2. Write a searching and fearless moral inventory of yourself.

Understanding the Fourth Step

The Fourth Step brings us to a specific course of action that the AA Big Book describes as "vigorous." It is a "personal house-cleaning which many of us had never attempted."[1] The Fourth Step strengthens the decision we made in the Third Step and helps us carry it out. According to the AA Big Book, unless we make a "strenuous effort to face, and to be rid of, the things in ourselves which [have] been blocking us," our decision to turn our will and our lives over to the care of God as we understand Him can "have little permanent effect."[2]

The Fourth Step is necessary to continue
the progress we have made in the first three Steps.

The AA Big Book uses the analogy of taking a business inventory to describe our Fourth Step work. An inventory is simply a list of everything the business owns, including all its raw materials, means of production, finished products, and so on. The purpose of an inventory is to identify the stock that is old, obsolete or spoiled so that it can be thrown out and replaced with stock that can be used or sold. Our moral inventory serves the same purpose. We want to find out what it is about ourselves that we need to "throw out" (in other words, to change) to have a more serene and productive life. To achieve that goal, we have to examine our lives to date and the negative characteristics that have caused us so much pain.

We prepare an inventory of who we are,
identifying the characteristics we want to keep
and those we want to change.

"We wish to look squarely at the unhappiness this [set of liabilities] has caused others and ourselves."[3] Our goal is to root out the causes of our living problems so that we can do something about them. We have embarked on a program of action that will restore us to sanity. That restoration, however, depends on our willingness to look at ourselves realistically and to endure the pain associated with facing what we have become. The fantasy of some "easier, softer way" that will allow us to avoid that pain has kept a number of us from completing this Step and from maintaining our recovery.

Many of us assumed that if we stopped our addictive behavior, all of our problems would be solved. Unfortunately, this wasn't true. By stopping that behavior, we *did* solve all those problems directly related to our active addiction or compulsion. We didn't get any more DWIs, for example. Nor did we get arrested for narcotic possession. We did not binge eat again, either.

Other problems persisted, however. Procrastination, resentments, rage, irresponsibility, grandiosity, and isolation continued to create problems for us in recovery. Problems that stemmed from our character defects did not go away just because we quit drinking, using, gambling, eating, or spending compulsively. "Liquor," says the AA Big Book was "but a symptom. So we had to get down to causes and conditions."[4] Once in recovery, we had to deal with these character defects regardless of the nature of our addiction or compulsion.

Our addictions were but a symptom.

The purpose of the Fourth Step is to identify those character defects. "We searched out the flaws in our make-up which [had] caused our failure."[5] The AA Big Book suggests that the inventory be written. Writing it down forces us to confront in black-and-white what is really there. Our inventory is moral because it concerns our behavior. It leads us back through a lifetime of actions that have caused pain for us and others and about which we feel shame and guilt. The purpose of this search is not humiliation and punishment, however, but freedom.

We seek release by discovering and exposing old secrets and by identifying the character defects that have caused our problems so that we never have to repeat the behavior. As with a business inventory, we are assessing the stock of our lives. We are categorizing what should be kept and what needs to be eliminated. "Nothing counted," says the AA Big Book, "but thoroughness and honesty."[6] Our courage in confronting our past behavior will be rewarded by a clearer picture of ourselves than we have ever had before. At last, we will know what it is that we have to work with.

"Our inventory entitles us to settle with the past."[7]

Inventory format and contents

The Fourth Step inventory is to be written. The AA Big Book and the Twelve and Twelve suggest a general outline that ought to be followed in writing a comprehensive Fourth Step. This outline is the one that I recommend to my sponsees with the understanding that they can modify it within reason in order to make the Step work for them. However, if they want to leave out part of the outline, we discuss the reason for that omission to be sure they aren't trying to avoid looking at some part of their lives. The main objectives are to be specific and thorough in covering the topics listed below.[8]

RESENTMENTS

"Being convinced that self, manifested in various ways, was what had defeated us, we considered its common manifestations. Resentment is the 'number one' offender," says the AA Big Book. "It destroys more alcoholics than anything else."[9] One problem with resentments is that they cause us to be unhappy. But there is a more serious problem. With alcoholics, "whose hope is the maintenance and growth of a spiritual experience, this business of resentment is infinitely grave. We found that it is fatal."[10] If we hold on to resentments, we will not be able to undergo the spiritual experience that protects us from a return to active alcoholism, addiction, or compulsive behavior.

Since resentments are the "number one offender," we ought to include a list of our resentments, to whom they are directed, the reason for each resentment, and what we did to contribute to that resentment. In this regard, the AA Big Book mentions a "grudge list" that should be "definite" and divided into four columns.

Our Fourth Step inventory
includes a list of our resentments.

The following table illustrates the format for listing resentments that is taken from page 65 of the AA Big Book, including the examples in the first three columns. The fourth column was added because its contents are described on page 67 of the Big Book (but the example used in the table was made up by the author to illustrate the principle). An explanation of how to complete each column follows the table.

Name of person or thing resented	Cause of the resentment (behavior of the person resented)	Area of life affected	Our character defects (and wrong behavior) that contributed to the situation
Mr. Brown	His attention to my wife	Sex relations	Anger and dishonesty: told lies about him to try to get him fired

1. In the first column of the table, write down the name of the person or thing for whom the resentment is held. It could be your wife, boss, employer, or college roommate. It could be the church, the government, or the company that didn't hire you. In preparing this inventory, it is probably better to complete this column first before you move on to the other columns. The chances are that if your inventory is thorough, this list will be a long one.

2. In the second column, list the cause of the resentment. What did the person, group, or institution do that made you angry and that you have not been able to let go of?

3. In the third column, list that area of your life that was hurt or threatened and so produced the resentment. According to the AA Big Book, some areas of life that might be affected and so give rise to resentments are self-esteem, security, personal relationships, sexual relations, and pride.[11]

4. In the fourth column, list what you did wrong and the character defect or defects that showed themselves in that action. What was *your* behavior that contributed to the situation that resulted in the resentment?[12] The AA Big Book specifically asks, "Where had we been selfish, dishonest, self-seeking and frightened?" In other words, "where were we to blame?"[13] In this column, we are "resolutely" looking for our own mistakes *only*. We ignore the other person's wrongs, no matter what they were.

Once you have completed this list of resentments, examine it for patterns of people, places, or things that you hold resentments toward (your family, employer, institutions, for example). Look also for patterns in the areas of your life that were affected (security, sexual relations, pride). Finally, identify recurring character defects and types of behavior that contributed to the situations that developed. What part have you played?

It is clear from the AA Big Book that we must be thorough in developing this list of resentments and that we are to look only at our own behavior—not at the other person's. Even if the other person were partially to blame for the problem, we look only at our role in it.

FEARS

The AA Big Book says, "We reviewed our fears thoroughly. We put them on paper, even though we had no resentment in connection with them. We asked ourselves why we had them."[14] Make a list of each fear you have and why you think you have it.

SEXUAL CONDUCT

We examine our sexual conduct. The AA Big Book says, "We reviewed our own [sexual] conduct over the years past. Where had we been selfish, dishonest, or inconsiderate? Whom had we hurt? Did we unjustifiably arouse jealousy, suspicion or bitterness? Where were we at fault, what should we have done instead? We got this all down on paper and looked at it."[15] We are specific about our sexual misconduct in whatever form.

THE SEVEN DEADLY SINS

We ask ourselves to what extent each of the Seven Deadly Sins could be applied to us. The AA Twelve and Twelve says, "To avoid falling into confusion over the names these defects should be called, let's take a universally recognized list of major human failings—the Seven Deadly Sins of pride, greed, lust, anger, gluttony, envy, and sloth [laziness]."[16] We list each of those failings that apply to us and how they have hurt us and others.

> *We look at each of the Seven Deadly Sins*
> *and how they apply to our lives.*

Since "selfishness—self-centeredness. . . is the root of our troubles," it makes sense in the Fourth Step to specifically address our grandiosity or self-will run riot. Self-will was one of the issues we dealt with in the Third Step. Now we have the opportunity to revisit that central problem of our lives by listing specific examples of grandiosity and self-centeredness and how they have hurt us and others. Usually, this family of character defects related to grandiosity is included under pride. Some examples may be: bragging, constructing a false image of ourselves, trying to be the center of attention, having to be right, not willing to admit it when we are wrong.

ASSETS

We make a list of our assets since an inventory includes a list of those things that should be kept as well as those things that should be thrown away. Furthermore, many of us had as distorted a view of our lack of assets as of our lack of liabilities. Since facing reality is our goal, we need to accept our strengths as well as our weaknesses.

Our inventory includes a list of our assets.

The AA Twelve and Twelve supports listing assets as part of the Fourth Step inventory. "The sponsor probably points out that the newcomer has some assets which can be noted [in the Fourth Step inventory] along with his liabilities. This tends to clear away morbidity and encourage balance. As soon as he begins to be more objective, the newcomer can fearlessly, rather than fearfully, look at his own defects."[17]

Finally, we double-check to see that we have left nothing important out of our inventory and that we have not kept any secrets. We want to be sure that we have included "the people we have hurt by our conduct."[18] AA The Big Book calls upon us to be "entirely honest."[19]

Our Fourth Step inventory must be "searching and fearless"
and include all our secrets.

Do all these suggestions make for a long Fourth Step? Yes. But if we are to be searching, fearless, and thorough, we can do little else.

Applying Step Four

Once taken, the Fourth Step has been completed unless another inventory is written in the future. The idea of conducting an ongoing inventory is not contained in this Step, but in Step Ten, "Continued to take personal inventory and when we were wrong promptly admitted it." Many Twelve Step members do take the

Fourth Step more than once as increasing awareness in recovery allows them to understand their character defects with greater depth and clarity.

Sponsor Guidelines for Working Step Four

Suggest that your sponsee do the readings and answer the questions listed under "Step Study." When your sponsee has completed this work, ask him or her to make an appointment with you to discuss the Step.

First meeting on Step Four

Based on the suggested readings, "Understanding the Fourth Step" in this chapter, and your own knowledge and experience, discuss Step Four with your sponsee. You may want to use the study questions or "Understanding the Fourth Step" as a discussion guide.

Remind your sponsee that his or her Fourth Step inventory should be safely hidden while it is being written. It can be a disaster if a spouse, co-worker, or child chances to find it (as sometimes happens).

**Keep your Fourth Step inventory
hidden in a very safe place.**

Sponsee questions

Sponsees seem to have more questions about Step Four than any other Step. Here are some of the common questions.

How long should it be?

It should be long enough to be "searching and fearless." The AA Big Book says, "If we have been thorough about our personal inventory, we have written down a lot."[20] There is no set number of pages.

What form should it be in?

The only requirement is that it be written. The AA Big Book suggests a form for the list of resentments which it calls "our grudge list."[21] Since the Big Book specifies the format for the resentment list, I favor following that format for that part of the Step. Otherwise, the Step can be in the form of an outline, a list, or a narrative as long as it is thorough.

Where should I keep it?

Keep it hidden somewhere that is very, very safe.

How long can I take on this Step?

The sooner you can complete it, the better. If the Fourth Step takes months, it is probably too long.

What if I'm not ready to take Step Four yet?

If you have taken Step Three, you are ready to begin working Step Four. Just because you don't want to write the inventory doesn't mean you aren't ready for the Step. Discuss this issue with your sponsor and look for the character defects that are blocking your progress: pride, self-will, fear, or whatever.

Do I have to do more than one Fourth Step?

It depends upon the thoroughness of your first Fourth Step. It appears that Bill Wilson did at least two Fourth Steps. His first Fourth and Fifth Steps were apparently taken in Towns Hospital in December 1934 during his last stay at that facility and following his spiritual experience.[22] In 1940, Bill took another Fifth Step with Father Ed Dowling, his spiritual advisor.[23] The second Fifth Step presumes a second Fourth Step.

Many of us have found that as "searching and fearless" as we had been in the first year or two of our recovery, we still had not plumbed the depths of our character defects. Later insights helped us see that our problems and character defects were more extensive than we had first realized. We needed to go back for a harder, deeper, more thorough look to take advantage of this new knowledge. We could see how our character defects had continued to hurt us, even in sobriety.

Later discussions

After the first meeting on Step Four, work regularly with your sponsee to help him or her stay focused on the Step and the inventory. Firm guidance is often needed. Beginning Step Four (much less completing it) is a frequent problem for sponsees. If properly done, the Fourth Step

· Is intensely painful and ego-deflating.
· Requires a written inventory that takes a significant amount of time to complete.
· Asks us to identify our character defects and to list the past behavior that has caused us problems.
· Brings us face-to-face with who we really are and what we have done.
· Describes our addiction or compulsion in vivid detail, forcing us to face the need for change.

When sponsees try to put off taking the Fourth Step

When sponsees try to put off taking the Fourth Step, it is sometimes helpful to discuss the issue of "I-don't-want-to-do-it" with them. Sponsees will confess, "I know I need to do the Fourth Step, but I don't want to" as if not *wanting* to take the Fourth Step made any difference. Many of us grew up basing our decisions on, "Do I want to do this or not?" It was only in recovery that we learned that the question is not, "Do I *want* to do this?" but "Do I *need* to do this?"

It doesn't matter whether or not we *want* to do the Fourth Step. Real life (as in restoration to sanity) requires us to do a number of things we would rather not do. The Fourth Step may be one of them. A Twelve Step saying that is helpful here is, "Do the next right thing." After the Third Step, the Fourth Step is the next right thing. Part of recovery is learning to do those things that are good for us whether or not we want to do them. This is an opportunity to "walk the talk."

While there is no precise timetable for taking this Step, significant delay should be challenged. When procrastination becomes severe, action needs to be taken to break the logjam. Some actions that have helped Twelve Step members take the Step are

1. Pray daily for the willingness and courage to complete the Step.
2. Reread the Fourth Step sections in the AA Big Book or equivalent and the Twelve and Twelve weekly.
3. Return to the Third Step for more work.
4. List the character defects you are hiding or exhibiting by resisting this Step.
5. List what it is that you are afraid of discovering about yourself in this Step.
6. Set a goal for completing different portions of the Step and report to your sponsor on the progress made.
7. Make a pact with a program friend who is also working the Fourth Step to meet together to write the inventory. Some program members have found that it is easier to sit in a room writing their inventory when they know a friend is doing the same thing in the next room.
8. Make sure that the written inventory is safely hidden.
9. Once the inventory has been started, make an appointment to take the Fifth Step as motivation to complete the inventory. (By contrast, some sponsors encourage their sponsees to write the Fourth Step without deciding who will hear it. In that way, they don't distort the inventory for fear of the Fifth Step to come.)

Taking Step Four

Step Four is unique in that there is no formal meeting in which it is finally taken. In a sense, the final meeting on the Fourth Step is the Fifth Step.

The Fourth Step has been taken when sponsees have met the following conditions:

1. They have completed a written inventory that they regard as "fearless and thorough."
2. They have listed and analyzed their resentments.
3. They have listed their fears.
4. They have reviewed their sexual conduct over the years, looking for the ways in which they had been selfish, dishonest, or inconsiderate, and identifying those whom they have hurt.
5. They have described how each of the Seven Deadly Sins listed in the AA Twelve and Twelve apply to them, including the "sin" of grandiosity (self-will run riot).
6. They have included somewhere on the inventory all the people they have harmed and the behavior that caused the harm. They have ignored the other person's role in creating the problem and have concentrated solely on their own role. They understand which character defect was responsible for the harm.
7. They have listed their assets.
8. They have not kept any secrets.
9. They have not left anything important out of the inventory.

It is worth reminding your sponsees that they are free to take the Fifth Step with anyone they please. The only guidelines in the AA Big Book are that the person chosen "be able to keep a confidence; that he [or she] fully understand and approve what we are driving at; that he [or she] will not try to change our plan."[24] If there are very deep secrets contained in the Fourth Step inventory that my sponsee cannot share with me, I suggest that he take the Fifth Step with a clergy member who understands what the Fifth Step is all about. The important thing is that *all* the secrets be shared.

In those cases where there is information that cannot be shared because of potential legal problems, I suggest that those specific examples be omitted from the Fifth Step my sponsee takes with me and that they be taken separately with a member of the clergy, a physician, or an attorney, where the confidence is protected by law.

13

Working Step Five

*Admitted to God, to ourselves, and to
another human being the exact nature of our wrongs.*

Timing of Step Five

The AA Big Book says, "When we decide who is to hear our story,
we waste no time." The Fifth Step should be worked immediately
after completion of the Fourth Step inventory.

Step Study

The following readings and questions are suggested for your sponsee as preparation for taking Step Five. Answers to the questions
can be found in the readings, in "Understanding the Fifth Step"
later in this chapter, and in your sponsee's personal experience.

Readings on the Step

1. Those pages in the AA Big Book that cover Step Five (pages
   72–75).
2. "Step Five" in the AA Twelve and Twelve (pages 55–62).

3. Other readings on the Step appropriate to your particular Twelve Step program: _____

_____

4. _____

_____

Questions about the Step

1. What are the objectives of the Fifth Step?
2. With whom do you want to take the Fifth Step?

*Bring your written Fourth Step inventory
to the Fifth Step meeting.*

Understanding the Fifth Step

In this Step, we admit to God, to ourselves, and to another person the exact nature of the wrongs we have committed as the result of our character defects. It is one thing to admit these wrongs and defects secretly to ourselves and quite another to write them down on paper and see them in black and white. It is still more humbling to admit them to another human being. That final admission makes them more real and more painful to us, while, at the same time, removes some of their power.

Key concepts

EGO DEFLATION

Step Five is another action Step and ego-deflating experience. The AA Twelve and Twelve tells us that "scarcely any Step is more necessary to longtime sobriety and peace of mind than this one."[1] Although all of the Twelve Steps deflate our egos, "when it comes to ego deflation, few Steps are harder to take than Five."[2] Yet the humility that comes with "confiding our defects to another human being" is one of the great rewards of this Step. According to the AA Twelve and Twelve, the word "humility" used in this sense means "a clear recognition of what and who we really are, followed by a sincere attempt to become what we could be."[3]

If we skip Step Five, we may not recover.

RIGOROUS HONESTY

In taking the Fifth Step, it is crucial to be "entirely honest." The AA Twelve and Twelve says, "Few muddled attitudes have caused us more trouble than holding back on Step Five. Some people are unable to stay sober at all; others will relapse periodically until they really clean house. Even A.A. oldtimers, sober for years, often pay dearly for skimping this Step."[4] This principle of rigorous honesty and the price for failing to practice it applies to other Twelve Step programs as well.

PATTERNS OF BEHAVIOR

The Fifth Step is more than just a cataloging of character defects and the negative consequences they caused. It is a search for patterns of thinking and behaving that have served us poorly. It is an effort to see clearly, with the help of another individual, what it is about ourselves that we need to change in order to be productive and happy. It is a searching and fearless examination of our lives in the loving presence of another human being and of God, however we may understand God. We are also admitting to ourselves what we have done. Many of us have lied to ourselves as often as we have lied to others.

The Fifth Step is an effort to see clearly
what it is about ourselves that we need to change.

CHOOSING WHO WILL HEAR STEP FIVE

The AA Twelve and Twelve describes the qualities of the person who should hear our Fifth Step as "someone who is experienced, who not only has stayed dry but has been able to surmount other serious difficulties. Difficulties, perhaps, like our own. This person may turn out to be one's sponsor, but not necessarily so."[5] The advantages of using a sponsor are that he or she knows something about us already, will know even more about us after the Fifth Step and so can help us work on our character defects, and is someone in whom we have confidence.

> *Our sponsor is the usual choice*
> *to hear our Fifth Step, but not always.*

The AA Twelve and Twelve cautions that even if your sponsor hears your Fifth Step, "It may turn, out, however, that you'll choose someone else for the more difficult and deeper revelations. This individual may be entirely outside of [the program] — for example, your clergyman or your doctor. For some of us, a complete stranger may prove the best bet."[6] The AA Big Book suggests that the person who hears our Fifth Step "be able to keep a confidence; that he fully understand and approve what we are driving at; that he will not try to change our plan."[7]

OBJECTIVES OF STEP FIVE

There are seven major objectives to Step Five:

1. To look honestly and completely at the wreckage of the past in order to identify those character defects that have gotten us into trouble. These are the defects we will need to work on in Steps Six and Seven.
2. To identify the specific instances and behaviors of the past that we want to put behind us so that we can begin anew with a clean slate. This part of the Fifth Step relates to the amends we will become willing to make in Step Eight and will actually make in Step Nine.

> *The Fifth Step is both*
> *humbling and freeing.*

3. To experience a needed sense of humility by admitting to God, to ourselves, and to another human being "the exact nature of our wrongs."

4. To feel guilt and remorse about what we have done to motivate us to do something about our character defects in the Steps to come.

5. To discover that we can both forgive others and receive forgiveness from them.[8]

6. To get rid of our terrible sense of isolation and loneliness.[9]

7. At the end of the Step, to relieve our guilt and reduce our shame. Once the Fifth Step is over, we need have no more guilt or shame about anything that we have done in the past. We are free.

Once the Fifth Step has been taken,
we have been completely honest with ourselves
and another human being.

The fruits of a well-executed Fifth Step are relief, forgiveness, and healing. A Twelve Step expression, "We are as sick as our secrets," applies here. The phrase means that when our secrets are kept secret, they fester and create problems for us. Only when they are revealed can they be healed. Step Five is about that healing. It is also about starting over. It is about having a new life. The AA Big Book says, "Once we have taken this step, withholding nothing, we are delighted. We can look the world in the eye. We can be alone at perfect peace and ease. Our fears fall from us. We begin to feel the nearness of our Creator. We may have had certain spiritual beliefs, but now we begin to have a spiritual experience. The feeling that the drink problem has disappeared will often come strongly. We feel we are on the Broad Highway, walking hand in hand with the Spirit of the Universe."[10]

With the Fifth Step,
we begin to have a spiritual experience.

Applying Step Five

The Fifth Step is unusual among the Steps in that it is the second part of the previous Step and it is taken entirely with a sponsor or with another individual. Once taken, it doesn't have to be taken again, unless another Fourth Step inventory is written later. On the other hand, the memory of the Fifth Step, the pain it brought, and the freedom it offered may be long remembered.

Sponsor Guidelines for Working Step Five

Suggest that your sponsee do the readings and answer the questions listed under "Step Study." When your sponsee has completed this work, ask him or her to make an appointment with you to discuss the Step.

First meeting on Step Five

Based on the suggested readings, "Understanding the Fifth Step" in this chapter, and your own knowledge and experience, discuss Step Five with your sponsee. You may want to use the study questions or "Understanding the Fifth Step" as a discussion guide.

Remind your sponsee that any information he or she chooses to share with you is *not* legally "privileged" the way it would be if it were shared with a doctor, lawyer, or member of the clergy. If your sponsee has something in his or her past that could be truly damaging if it were revealed through subpoena or otherwise, or if he or she is involved in an ongoing crime that would legally have to be reported to the authorities, he or she may prefer to discuss those aspects of the Fourth Step inventory with a member of the clergy or a lawyer who understands the purpose of the Fifth Step.

Taking Step Five

How your sponsee takes the Fifth Step is important. A well-structured Fifth Step experience can strengthen the Step's power to motivate change and to bring about transformation. Careful planning can add to its effect—to the feelings of freedom and release that often accompany completion of the Step.

A well-planned Fifth Step
will be more effective for your sponsee.

More important than the format of the Fifth Step experience, however, is the authenticity of the sponsor in listening carefully and closely to his or her sponsee's inventory. The vulnerability we all assume as sponsees in taking the Fifth Step with another human being is both awesome and inspiring. If we were searching and fearless in our inventory, the resulting Fifth Step is completely revealing. We will have exposed our deepest secrets to another person, trusting as we have never trusted before.

To hear another person's Fifth Step is an honor and a privilege. It is a moment of intimacy, openness, and trust—the likes of which most humans rarely experience. In the final analysis, the Fifth Step is a three-way experience among you, your sponsee, and God.

General guidelines for sponsors

SET ASIDE PLENTY OF TIME

A thorough Fifth Step can easily take five hours or more. The AA Big Book says, "We have a written inventory and we are prepared for a long talk."[11] If the inventory is "searching and fearless," it cannot be dealt with briefly. So it is important not to rush the Fifth Step even if your sponsee would like to do so. If the session runs past the allotted time, reschedule its completion for another day. Try to arrange it so that there are no interruptions. Remind your sponsee that the Fifth Step includes an hour of solitary meditation after you have heard his or her inventory.

Allow plenty of time for the Fifth Step.

TAILOR THE PROCESS TO YOUR SPONSEE

What is right for one person is not necessarily right for another. Ask your Higher Power to guide you to do and say the right thing. Listen to your intuition.

Ask your Higher Power
to guide you in the process.

TRY TO HELP YOUR SPONSEE
TAKE THE STEP WITH FEELING

Not everyone in a Twelve Step program will agree with this suggestion. It has been the experience of many of us, however, that the Step is more effective when a sponsee can feel the pain, anger, sadness, loneliness, guilt, and shame associated with his or her character defects and inappropriate behavior of the past. By avoiding those feelings, a sponsee can use intellectual distance to counter the power of the Step and the depth of the humility it is designed to produce.

Not every sponsor feels comfortable dealing with feelings, and certainly every sponsee does not. If you are not comfortable, don't worry about it.

Try to help your sponsee take the Fifth Step
emotionally as well as intellectually.

CHOOSE AN APPROPRIATE SETTING
AND HAVE BASIC TEXT AVAILABLE

Choose a location that is quiet, comfortable, and free from distractions, and have available copies of the basic text of your Twelve Step program and the Twelve and Twelve equivalent.

Specific guidelines for sponsors

There are many ways to stage a Fifth Step. The suggestions contained in this chapter will produce a structured format that can lead to a very rewarding experience. If all these proposed activities do not fit your style, however, use only those that appeal to

you. Some sponsors are more comfortable with structure and rit-
ual than others.

A well-structured Fifth Step
adds to its power.

1. Start by asking your sponsee how he or she feels. Most sponsees experience a great deal of fear in anticipation of taking
   the Fifth Step, and it helps to get that fear out into the open.
   If you are feeling some fear yourself, admit to that fear (as
   well as joy at the prospect of your sponsee taking this important Step). There is usually fear involved in *hearing* a Fifth
   Step as well as in taking it.

2. Pause for a moment of silent meditation followed by the
   Serenity Prayer. (Suggest to your sponsee that he or she take
   advantage of the silence to ask God for the strength and
   courage to be honest and thorough in the Step. Ask your
   Higher Power for guidance and assistance.)

Begin the Fifth Step with a moment of silent meditation
and the Serenity Prayer.

3. If your sponsee is an alcoholic, turn to page 72 of the AA Big
   Book (this is where the Fifth Step begins). Read the entire
   Fifth Step as it is presented in the Big Book *down to* the last
   paragraph on page 75 (do not read the last paragraph yet). If
   your sponsee is not an alcoholic, substitute a Fifth Step reading from the basic text of your Twelve Step program. For the
   reading from the AA Big Book, I alternate reading paragraphs
   with my sponsee, and I read the first paragraph. The reason is
   that the last paragraph is particularly powerful for a sponsee
   to read. By alternating, we share the reading burden and
   make this aspect of the preparation a partnership experience.

Read with your sponsee the passage on the Fifth Step
from the AA Big Book or equivalent.

4. Renew your pledge of confidentiality to reassure your sponsee that everything he or she says will be kept confidential.

5. Have your sponsee begin his or her Fifth Step based on the written Fourth Step inventory. Some sponsors ask their sponsees to read the written inventory so that nothing is left out. Others ask them to use the inventory as an outline for their discussion. The preference is yours or your sponsee's. The following are some guidelines for this phase of the process:

A.   Look for repetitive patterns of behavior and point them out if your sponsee doesn't see them.

> **Look for repetitive, self-destructive patterns of behavior.**

B. If you are comfortable with it, do a mini-Fifth Step of your own during the process, never trying to "top" your sponsee with stories, but to share similar experiences so that he or she won't feel so alone or unique.

C. Ask your sponsee to list the character defects that continually seem to cause the most trouble (if they are not clear from the presentation).

D. If your sponsee has left out any character defects you are aware of, ask about them. In particular, inquire about grandiosity if it hasn't been included. Have resentments been listed and analyzed? Have fears been listed as well as people who have been harmed? Review the Seven Deadly Sins if you think they haven't been covered (pride, greed, lust, anger, gluttony, envy, and sloth). Not every "sin" will necessarily apply to each person, however, to such a degree that it constitutes a major character defect.

E. If your sponsee fails to list his or her assets, then ask him or her to do so, since an inventory includes both those things we need to get rid of as well as those things we want to keep.[12]

> **The AA Twelve and Twelve suggests that sponsees include a list of assets in their Fifth Step.**

6. Once your sponsee has completed the inventory, ask if there is anything else that he or she remembers that wasn't written down but which should be included. The inventory is to be "searching and fearless"; you cannot overemphasize the need for honesty. The idea of the Fifth Step is to enable us to begin anew with a clean slate, *if we have left nothing out*. Encourage your sponsee to be completely open so that he or she can walk away from this Step a free human being.

   **Ask your sponsee if anything has
   been omitted from the Step.**

7. Instruct your sponsee to keep the Fourth Step inventory because he or she will need it for Steps Eight and Nine. Anything for which your sponsee owes an amend should have been covered in the Fourth and Fifth Steps. Not all sponsors agree with keeping the inventory. Some suggest that the Fourth Step be torn up or burned as a symbol of freedom from the wreckage of the past.

8. The last paragraph on page 75 of the AA Big Book describes what your sponsee should do after completing the Fifth Step with you. It suggests that he or she

   A. Return home.

   B. Be quiet for an hour.

   C. Review what has been revealed to him or her in the Fifth Step.

   D. Review the first Five Steps.

   E. Thank God for the spiritual progress that has been made ("for knowing [God] better," as the AA Big Book puts it).

   F. Ask himself or herself if there is anything that was omitted in taking those Steps.

Explain that the Step *has not been worked until these actions have been taken*. Urge him or her to follow through on this last part of the Step *and to call you at the end of the hour of meditation* to discuss any additional insights or thoughts that developed.

9. Tell your sponsee that what has happened in the past now belongs to the past. His or her slate is clean. Your sponsee is free.

10. If it feels appropriate for both you and your sponsee, suggest that you close with a prayer. Invite your sponsee to follow yours with one of his or her own. After you have said, "Amen," pause in case your sponsee wishes to make his or her own prayer.

11. Close by saying the Lord's Prayer together, if appropriate. Otherwise, use the Serenity Prayer.

Close the Fifth Step with a prayer.

Fifth Step Outline

The following outline may prove helpful during the course of hearing a Fifth Step. Use this page as a guide during the Step.

1. Ask your sponsee how he or she feels.

2. Have a moment of silent meditation followed by the Serenity Prayer.

3. For alcoholics, turn to page 72 of the AA Big Book. Read the first paragraph and ask your sponsee to read the next. Alternate reading down to the last paragraph on page 75. For other Twelve Step Fellowships, select a Fifth Step reading from your basic text.

4. Renew your pledge of confidentiality.

5. Have your sponsee begin reading or discussing his or her Fourth Step inventory. During the course of the inventory, look for repetitive patterns of behavior to point out if your sponsee hasn't seen them. Also check for these items:
   · Did your sponsee specify those character defects that have caused the most trouble?
   · Were resentments listed and analyzed?
   · Were fears listed?
   · Were the Seven Deadly Sins covered where applicable?

· Were the names of those individuals who were harmed listed along with the deeds that caused the harm?

6. Ask your sponsee to list his or her assets.

7. Ask if there is anything else that needs to be included to complete the Step.

8. Read the last paragraph on page 76 of the AA Big Book. Explain that the Step has not been worked until these actions have been taken.

9. Ask your sponsee to call you after he or she has completed the hour of meditation called for in the last paragraph on page 76 of the AA Big Book.

10. Tell your sponsee that what has happened in the past now belongs to the past.

11. If appropriate for your sponsee, close with individual prayers and then with the Lord's Prayer or Serenity Prayer.

14

Working
Step Six

*Were entirely ready to have God
remove all these defects of character.*

Timing of Step Six

We are ready to begin Step Six immediately after completing Step
Five. Step Five, however, has not been worked until we have thoroughly reviewed our work to date. The AA Big Book puts it this
way: "Taking this book down from our shelf we turn to the page
which contains the twelve steps. Carefully reading the first five
proposals we ask if we have omitted anything, for we are building
an arch through which we shall walk a free man [or woman] at
last. Is our work solid so far? Are the stones properly in place?
Have we skimped on the cement put into the foundation? Have
we tried to make mortar without sand? If we can answer to our
satisfaction, we then look at *Step Six.*"[1]

Step Study

The following readings and questions are suggested for your
sponsee as preparation for taking Step Six. Answers to the
questions can be found in the readings, in "Understanding the
Sixth Step" later in this chapter, and in your sponsee's personal
experience.

Readings on the Step

1. The page in the AA Big Book that covers Step Six (page 76).
2. "Step Six" in the AA Twelve and Twelve (pages 63–69).
3. Other readings on the Step appropriate to your particular Twelve Step program: ———————————————————

————————————————————————————————

4. ————————————————————————————————

————————————————————————————————

Questions about the Step

1. What is meant by "defects of character"?
2. What are the defects of character that you identified in your Fourth Step inventory that need to be removed?
3. How have these defects caused you problems in the past, and what problems are they causing you today?
4. Are you willing to give up the defects of character that give you pleasure or provide some other kind of reward?
5. If you could have these defects of character removed right now, would you? If not, why?
6. What do you get out of keeping these defects of character?
7. What does it mean to be "entirely ready"?
8. If you are not "entirely ready," how ready are you?
9. Are you willing to ask for God's help in this Step, recognizing that you cannot remove your defects of character by self-will alone?
10. Do you believe that the removal of your character defects is part of your restoration to sanity?
11. If you are not now willing to have these defects removed, how can you become willing?

Activities for the Step

1. Pray for willingness to take this Step.

Understanding the Sixth Step

According to the AA Twelve and Twelve, "This is the Step that separates the men from the boys."[2] And, it should be added, the women from the girls. Step Six addresses the issue of our readiness to have removed the defects of character that we identified in Step Four and that we admitted to God, to ourselves, and to another human being in Step Five. After the rigors of the two preceding Steps, this Step seems, at first glance, to be quick and easy. Not much is required in terms of specific action, yet a great deal is required emotionally and spiritually.

This Step asks us whether or not we are entirely willing to have God remove all our defects of character. Are we willing, in other words, to behave differently from the way we have in the past? Are we willing to change ourselves and to be changed? The AA Big Book puts it this way, "Are we now ready to let God remove from us all the things which we have admitted are objectionable? Can [God] now take them all—every one?"[3] If we are not willing, we are faced again with self-will. We are once more insisting on our own way, even when that way is destructive.

Step Six is about willingness.

As we have experienced before, if we do not recognize a problem, we cannot solve it. Step Six allows us to see the problem. It focuses our attention on our unwillingness to give up the defects of character that we enjoy (such as self-righteous anger and feeling superior toward others).[4] This recognition of the problem enables us to do something about it. "At the very least, we shall have to come to grips with some of our worst character defects and take action toward their removal as quickly as we can," suggests the AA Twelve and Twelve. "Delay is dangerous, and rebellion may be fatal. This is the exact point at which we abandon limited objectives, and move toward God's will for us."[5]

Self-will in the form of our character defects causes a lot of pain that we could otherwise avoid. A review of our Fourth Step inventory is proof enough of that. Even more important, our character defects can lead us back to our addictions or compulsions and their nightmarish consequences. The AA Twelve and Twelve describes our character defects as "flaws which must be dealt with to prevent a retreat into alcoholism."[6] It is urgent, therefore, that we deal with these defects of character.

Our character defects cause us pain
and can lead us back to our addictions or compulsions.

Given that urgency, Step Six can be confusing because it seems to demand perfection. The phrase "entirely ready" is the sticking point. Who among us is entirely ready to have our defects of character removed? If we are not entirely ready, have we truly taken this Step? The AA Twelve and Twelve offers this interpretation: "The key words 'entirely ready' underline the fact that we want to aim at the very best we know or can learn. "How many of us have this degree of readiness? In an absolute sense practically nobody has it. The best we can do, with all the honesty that we can summon, is to *try* to have it. Even then the best of us will discover to our dismay that there is always a sticking point, a point at which we say, 'No, I can't give this up yet.'"[7]

The AA Twelve and Twelve assures us, "Only Step One, where we made the 100 percent admission we were powerless over alcohol can be practiced with absolute perfection. The remaining eleven Steps state perfect ideals. They are goals toward which we look, and the measuring sticks by which we estimate our progress. Seen in this light, Step Six is still difficult, but not at all impossible. The only urgent thing is that we make a beginning, and keep trying."[8]

We cannot remove our character defects
without the help of our Higher Power.

Applying Step Six

Step Six is never completed because we cannot achieve a perfect willingness to have God remove our defects of character. The development of more and more willingness to have our defects of character removed is a lifetime process. Some days we are more willing than others. On those days more of our defects of character are removed, or they are removed to a greater extent. As with Step Three, we can turn it over and take it back in an endless cycle of my-will/Thy-will indecision. With both Steps, pray for willingness.

Pray for willingness.

The impossibility of achieving the Step perfectly, however, does not mean that we should not try to do it as completely as we can. The AA Twelve and Twelve says that the difference in the Sixth Step between "the boys and the men" and the girls and the women is "the difference between striving for a self-determined objective and for the perfect objective which is one of God."[9] While we can't practice this Step perfectly, we can practice it with courage and discipline, striving for the ideal of complete readiness. Our character defects cause us pain and suffering no matter how much we love them. The more of them and their manifestations we can be rid of, the happier we will be.

Sponsor Guidelines for Working Step Six

Suggest that your sponsee do the readings and answer the questions listed under "Step Study." When your sponsee has completed this work, ask him or her to make an appointment with you to discuss the Step.

First meeting on Step Six

Based on the suggested readings, "Understanding the Sixth Step" in this chapter, and your own knowledge and experience, discuss

Step Six with your sponsee. You may want to use the study questions or "Understanding the Sixth Step" as a discussion guide.

Later discussions

Assist your sponsees as they wrestle with willingness and their fear of what it would be like to lose their character defects. Remind them that "entirely willing" is an ideal and that the Step can be considered taken when they have achieved a practical willingness that will enable them to move on to Step Seven.

If they remain unwilling, suggest that they ask God to help them be willing.

Being "entirely willing" is an ideal.

Taking Step Six

Step Six may be the most difficult of all the Steps to take from a technical standpoint because of the words "entirely ready." Almost no one is "entirely ready" to have his or her defects of character removed. Given that fact, at what point are we to pronounce the Step "taken" even though its requirements have not strictly been met? The answer is not easy.

The basic criteria that I have developed for having taken Step Six are listed below. I discuss each of these points with my sponsees. When they can tell me that they have met them all, I am satisfied that they have taken the Step. These are the criteria:

1. They can name their character defects that need to be removed and know which seem to be the most difficult for them.
2. They have achieved a degree of willingness that has opened them to being changed. While not necessarily "entirely ready" to have their defects removed, they are now more open to the idea than closed to it.
3. They are willing to pray daily for the willingness to have their defects of character removed.

4. They recognize that while they must do the legwork in removing their character defects, the ultimate removal is not by their own resources, but by the grace of God.

5. They are willing to have God remove the defects in whatever way God sees fit to remove them. They will not insist on defining the ways in which the defects will be removed or in setting a timetable. In this sense, they have turned their will and lives over to the care of God. (They have reaffirmed the Third Step.)

6. They recognize that the removal of their character defects is part of their restoration to sanity. (They have reaffirmed the Second Step.)

After my sponsee has answered each of these questions in the affirmative, I suggest that we close our meeting with a prayer. I pray for my sponsee's willingness to have his defects of character removed and for willingness to have my own removed. With the understanding that the Sixth Step is never completed, I consider that my sponsee has taken the Step.

15

Working
Step Seven

Humbly asked Him to remove our shortcomings.

Timing of Step Seven

The AA Big Book does not discuss the timing of Step Seven except to say that it is taken "when ready." It would seem, however, that as soon as your sponsee has worked the Sixth Step and is ready to have God remove his or her character defects, he or she would ask God to do so. Therefore, it is appropriate for your sponsee to begin Step Seven immediately after working Step Six.

Step Study

The following readings and questions are suggested for your sponsee as preparation for taking Step Seven. Answers to the questions can be found in the readings, in "Understanding the Seventh Step" later in this chapter, and in your sponsee's personal experience.

Readings on the Step

1. The page in the AA Big Book that covers Step Seven (page 76).
2. "Step Seven" in the AA Twelve and Twelve (pages 70–76).

3. Other readings on the Step appropriate to your particular Twelve Step program: _____

_____

4. _____

_____

Questions about the Step

1. What does it mean to "humbly ask"?
2. What is humility?
3. What are "our shortcomings"?

Understanding the Seventh Step

The AA Twelve and Twelve tells us that "the whole emphasis of Step Seven is on humility."[1] We first looked at humility in the Third Step when we made the decision to turn our will and our lives over to the care of God. "The attainment of greater humility is the foundation principle of each of A.A.'s Twelve Steps. For without some degree of humility, no alcoholic can stay sober at all. Nearly all A.A.'s have found, too, that unless they develop much more of this precious quality than may be required just for sobriety, they still haven't much chance of becoming truly happy. Without it, they cannot live to much useful purpose, or, in adversity, be able to summon the faith that can meet any emergency."[2]

Step Seven is about humility.

Bill Wilson explains humility in this way, "As long as we placed self-reliance first, a genuine reliance upon a Higher Power was out of the question. That basic ingredient of all humility, a desire to seek and do God's will, was missing."[3] Humility, we discover, is not something to be resisted, but something to be accepted, even embraced. "Our eyes begin to open to the immense values which have come straight out of painful ego-puncturing."[4]

Humility is putting God's agenda
ahead of our own.

But the process, writes Bill Wilson, "was unbelievably painful. It was only by repeated humiliations that we were forced to learn something about humility."[5] As time went by, however, we realized that there was a more effective way to achieve it. "We saw we needn't always be bludgeoned and beaten into humility. It could come quite as much from our voluntary reaching for it as it could from unremitting suffering. A great turning point in our lives came when we sought for humility as something we really wanted, rather than as something we *must* have."[6] The process, however, is not a quick one. ". . . To gain a vision of humility as the avenue to true freedom of the human spirit, to be willing to work for humility as something to be desired for itself, takes most of us a long, long time."[7]

Taking the Third Step was a bold example of spiritual humility because it was a decision to turn our will and our lives over to the care of God. With the Seventh Step, we have an opportunity to put that decision into practice by asking God to do something specific for us: remove our defects of character. By asking God *humbly* to do so, we are saying, "Thy will, not mine, be done" in the timing and the manner of their removal.

Whether God will remove our defects instantly or slowly or ask us to labor mightily to remove them ourselves is up to God. We do not get to dictate the terms, conditions, or timetable by which the defects will be removed. Being humble is being open to the will of God however that will might be expressed. It is also recognizing that we are not able to remove these defects without God's help. They are too much for us acting alone.

The manner and timing of the
removal of our character defects
are up to God, not us.

Applying Step Seven

Step Seven is a Step we apply daily in our lives. As with Step Six, the Seventh Step is never completed. The removal of some of our character defects and the reduction of others is a lifelong process.

Sponsor Guidelines for Working Step Seven

Suggest that your sponsee do the readings and answer the questions listed under "Step Study." When your sponsee has completed this work, ask him or her to make an appointment with you to discuss the Step.

Step Seven is applied daily for life.

First meeting on the Step

Based on the suggested readings, "Understanding the Seventh Step" in this chapter, and your own knowledge and experience, discuss Step Seven with your sponsee. You may want to use the study questions or "Understanding the Step" as a discussion guide.

Taking Step Seven

Discuss the meaning of Step Seven with your sponsee, including his or her understanding of the word "humility." When you have finished, ask your sponsee: "Are you now willing to ask God to remove your defects of character?"

If the answer is yes, ask your sponsee to turn to page 76 of the AA Big Book and read aloud the Seventh Step prayer contained in the second paragraph. If your Fellowship is not AA, have your sponsee read the Seventh Step prayer from this page (it follows in the next paragraph), or make up his or her own version as long as it contains the intended central idea.

The Seventh Step prayer is as follows: "My Creator, I am now willing that you should have all of me, good and bad. I pray that you now remove from me every single defect of character which stands in the way of my usefulness to you and my fellows. Grant me strength, as I go out from here, to do your bidding. Amen."[8]

After your sponsee has finished saying the prayer (or his or her version of it), your sponsee has taken Step Seven.

16

Working
Step Eight

*Made a list of all persons we had harmed,
and became willing to make amends to them all.*

Timing of Step Eight

About the timing of Step Eight, the AA Big Book says, "Now we need more action, without which we find that 'Faith without works is dead.' Let's look at *Steps Eight and Nine.*"[1] Your sponsee is ready to begin the Eighth Step after working Step Seven.

Step Study

The following readings and questions are suggested for your sponsee as preparation for taking Step Eight. Answers to the questions can be found in the readings, in "Understanding the Eighth Step" later in this chapter, and in your sponsee's personal experience.

Readings on the Step

1. The page in the AA Big Book that covers Step Eight (page 76).
2. "Step Eight" in the AA Twelve and Twelve (pages 77–82).

3. Other readings on the Step appropriate to your particular Twelve Step program: _____

_____

4. _____

_____

Questions about the Step

1. What does the term "harm" mean in this Step?
2. What does it mean to "make amends" to someone?
3. What is the role of forgiveness in the amends process?
4. Why must we be willing to make amends to *all* those we have harmed? Can't there be any exceptions?
5. What is the purpose of this Step?

Activities for the Step

1. Prepare a list of all those you have harmed. The names should come from your Fourth Step inventory. For each name on the list
   · Include the exact nature of the harm.
   · Identify the character defect that led to the harm: envy, jealousy, greed, grandiosity, or dishonesty, for example.
2. Pray for the willingness to make amends to all the people you've harmed.
3. Pray for the willingness to forgive those you have harmed for whatever ways they may have hurt you.

Understanding the Eighth Step

Step Eight is concerned with our personal relationships. It is an examination of how we have dealt with people in the past and, more specifically, how we have harmed them. This Step is the basis for developing a more productive and satisfactory way of dealing with others. The AA Twelve and Twelve says that Step

Eight "is the beginning of the end of isolation from our fellows and from God."[2]

Step Eight is about improving
our personal relationships.

According to the AA Twelve and Twelve, Steps Eight and Nine involve this process: "First, we take a look backward and try to discover where we have been at fault; next we make a vigorous attempt to repair the damage we have done; and third, having thus cleaned away the debris of the past, we consider how, with our newfound knowledge of ourselves, we may develop the best possible relations with every human being we know. "This is a very large order."[3]

Key concepts

MAKING AN AMENDS LIST

The Eighth Step suggests that we prepare an amends list. This list should be in writing and include the names of all the people we have harmed who appeared in our Fourth Step inventory. We add the names of anyone we had forgotten or overlooked. Have we included everyone whom we can remember? Is there anyone to whom we did something that we still feel guilty about? The AA Twelve and Twelve says that we "ransack memory for the people to whom we have given offense. To put a finger on the nearby and most deeply damaged ones shouldn't be hard to do. Then, as year by year we walk back through our lives as far as memory will reach, we shall be bound to construct a long list of people who have, to some extent or other, been affected."[4] Our objective is to make the list as complete as possible.

Our amends list begins with the
names on our Fourth Step inventory.

In making the amends list and describing the harm done, follow the guidelines in the AA Twelve and Twelve. They suggest that we

1. Conduct "a deep and honest search of our [past] motives and actions."

2. Reject the idea that we might have harmed no one. Such is not the case with someone who is drinking, using, or engaging in compulsive behavior. If we think we have harmed no one, we are purposefully forgetting.

3. Focus on our own behavior, not on the other person's behavior. It is tempting to avoid looking at the wrongs we have done to others by looking instead at the real or imagined wrongs they have done to us. We forget that our addictive or compulsive behavior often aggravated the defects of others and led them to actions they would not otherwise have taken.

FORMAT OF THE AMENDS LIST

The format of our list will look something like the following table. Each column contains information that will be useful to us in this Step or in the Ninth Step. The column headings are explained in the paragraphs that follow:

Name of person harmed	Relationship	Nature of the harm	Character defects that caused the harm	Am I willing to forgive the other person?
Erik	Employer	Stole $1,000	Dishonesty and greed	Yes
Cal	Nephew	Tried to control	Grandiosity	Yes

1. In the first column ("Name of person harmed"), write down the name of each person harmed. When you find that the harm you did to another person was not nearly as great as the harm he or she did to you, include that person's name anyway. These are the individuals to whom you will make the amends in Step Nine.

2. In column two ("Relationship"), describe that person's relationship to you (brother, parent, spouse, employer, employee, and so on).

3. In column three ("Nature of the harm"), enter the exact nature of the harm you caused. What was your behavior and how did it hurt the other person? The ways in which we have harmed people are many and varied. The AA Twelve and Twelve defines harm as "physical, mental, emotional, or spiritual damage to people."[5] Some examples it offers are: a consistently bad temper, lying, cheating, selfishness, irresponsibility, callousness, being cold to other people, impatience, being critical, and attempts to dominate others.[6] These are the behaviors for which you will make amends in the Ninth Step.

> *Our amends list is focused on*
> *what we have done to others.*

4. In column four ("Character defects that caused the harm"), write down your character defects that caused the harm listed in column three. Since part of our recovery is the elimination or reduction of these defects of character, we need to see again how destructive they have been for us. The AA Twelve and Twelve says, "We can go far beyond those things which were superficially wrong with us, to see those flaws which were basic, flaws which sometimes were responsible for the whole pattern of our lives. Thoroughness, we have found, will pay—and pay handsomely."[7]

5. In looking at these past relationships, we ask ourselves whether or not we are willing to forgive those people who have harmed us. We have no right to ask others to forgive us if we are not willing to forgive. In the last column ("Am I willing to forgive the other person?"), enter yes or no.

> *In order to ask others to forgive us,*
> *we have to be willing to forgive.*

While we are constructing our lists, we do not look at the type of amends we have to make or at the consequences of those amends. In some cases, it might not be feasible, possible, or even advisable to make amends, for example, if it would destroy another person's reputation. But those issues are reserved for Step Nine. What is necessary in this Step is to become *willing* to make amends to *everyone on the list regardless of the consequences to us.* Our objective is to stay focused on that goal and not use our fear of making amends as an excuse for omitting someone's name from the list.

MAKING AMENDS TO THEM ALL

Once the list is complete, we face the major challenge of the Step. Are we willing to make amends to *all* these people, regardless of the personal cost? Only when we can answer "yes" has the Step been taken.

Step Eight is about willingness and ego-deflation. Once again, we revisit the painful adventures of the past in which our character defects have manifested themselves. Once again, we own up to the wreckage our self-will has caused us. But now it is time to admit our faults, mistakes, and character defects not only to God, to ourselves, and to another human being, *but also to the very individuals whom we have harmed.* We have to make amends for what we have done. In the process, we accept both responsibility for, and the consequences of, our past behavior. Only in that way can we find freedom. There is no other way to put the guilt and shame of the past behind us and ensure that we will not behave that way again.

> *In Step Eight, our willingness to make amends*
> *is without exception.*

FORGIVING THOSE WHO HAVE HARMED US

Next to developing the willingness to make amends, the hardest part of this Step may be developing the willingness to forgive. Forgiveness is a central element of the Step.[8] If we are going to ask forgiveness of others, we must be willing to offer it ourselves. So we look back at those who have harmed us and whom we have harmed in return—and we forgive them. We forgive them *no matter what they have done to us.* We forgive them so that we can be free.

Step Eight
is about forgiving and being forgiven.

Hate binds us; love frees us. Those whom we hate or hold resentments against, we remain tied to. We are enslaved by our resentments, freed by our loves. When we can forgive, we convert slavery into freedom. If forgiveness doesn't come easily, we pray about it and talk about it until it does come. We pray daily for the object of our resentment, even if we don't mean it at first. It is through forgiveness that we can finally let go of the past and begin anew.

Applying Step Eight

We do an Eighth Step every time we do a Fourth and Fifth Step, assuming that we have recognized new people we have harmed or new ways in which we have harmed them. The Eighth Step is not a Step we apply daily in our lives because it concerns the past. The fundamental principle of the Step (being willing to make amends) is contained in Step Ten. Step Ten reads, "Continued to take personal inventory and when we were wrong promptly admitted it."

Sponsor Guidelines for Working Step Eight

Suggest that your sponsee do the readings and answer the questions listed under "Step Study." When your sponsee has completed this work, ask him or her to make an appointment with you to discuss the Step.

First meeting on the Step

Based on the suggested readings, "Understanding the Eighth Step" in this chapter, and your own knowledge and experience, discuss Step Eight with your sponsee. You may want to use the study questions or "Understanding the Step" as a discussion guide.

After the discussion, ask your sponsee to prepare a written amends list. Suggest that he or she follow the format contained in "Understanding the Eighth Step."

Sponsee questions

Sponsees often have questions about Step Eight. Here are some of the common ones:

Do I have to list everybody
I've ever harmed?

Include all those you have harmed. Of course, you can't remember everyone you have ever harmed. List those you can remember that were significant but don't be obsessive about it. "A quiet, objective view"[9] is our goal. If you have any doubts, include the name.

What if I don't know
where they are now?

It doesn't matter. This is a list of people you have harmed, not a list of people you have harmed and can get in touch with easily.

What if they hurt me
more than I hurt them?

If you have harmed them, their names belong on the list. It doesn't matter whether or not they have harmed you. Your focus in this amends list is on what *you* have done. It is on cleaning up your side of the street. Their side of the street is not your concern at this moment.

What if I don't want to make amends
to them or they don't deserve it?

Put their names on the list anyway. The first part of the Step is to make a list of all those you have harmed. The second part of the Step (being willing to make amends to them all) comes after you've made the list.

What if I got drunk at a party and did or
said something that was very bad to a
blind date and he or she was also drunk
and I never saw that person again?

If you remember the incident and harm was done, include the person's name on the list. Your goal is to clean up the wreckage of the past. If there is a lot of wreckage, there are a lot of names. This Step is about making a list and about being willing. It is not about making the amend, so it doesn't matter whether or not you know where they are.

What if I remember what happened but not
the name of the person I've harmed?

List the incident and describe it.

This could be a very long list.
It could take me a long time to write it.

That's true.

What if I will get in serious trouble
if I make an amend?

This Step is not about making an amend to the person harmed. It is not even about deciding what type of amend you ought to make. It is only about making a list of those you have harmed and becoming willing to make amends to them all. It is in the Ninth Step that you will consider the type of amend that needs to be made. So put the person's name on the list and the nature of the harm that could get you in trouble if you made an amend.

Why do I have to list
the specific character defect?

There are several reasons. The first is that you are trying to get rid of your character defects, so it will be helpful to see how they present themselves in your life. The second is that it will help you see how much harm your character defects have caused you and others. Seeing the consequences of your past behavior will help motivate you to change it in the future.

*What if I'm not willing
to forgive someone on the list?*

Try these suggestions:

· Focus on your contribution to the harm that was done. What was *your* role in it? Try to accept responsibility for your part.
· Reread the homework assignments weekly.
· Pray daily for the problem person (whether or not you mean it), for the willingness to forgive, and for the resentment to be taken away.

Taking Step Eight

An Eighth Step resembles a Fifth Step in that it is admitting to another person the exact nature of the harm we have caused. In this last meeting on the Step, ask your sponsee to discuss his or her amends list with you. For *each person* on the list, ask your sponsee to

· Give the person's name and relationship (brother, sister, teacher, neighbor, employer, and so on).
· Describe the behavior that caused the harm which now requires an amend.
· Identify the specific character defects that manifested themselves in that behavior.
· Describe how he or she feels about the behavior now.
· Confirm that he or she is willing to forgive that person for his or her contribution, if any, to the harm that resulted.
· Confirm that he or she is willing to make amends to that person regardless of the personal cost of doing so. The exact amend, however, should not be discussed at this time.

If your sponsee is willing to make amends and to forgive the person, move to the next name on the list. If your sponsee is not willing to do the above, discuss why.

After your sponsee has finished discussing all the names on the list, reconfirm that he or she is willing to make amends to *all* those harmed *without regard to the consequences to himself or herself*. Until your sponsee is willing to make amends to *everyone* on the list and *to forgive them*, the Step has not been taken.

17

Working
Step Nine

*Made direct amends to such people wherever possible,
except when to do so would injure them or others.*

Timing of Step Nine

Regarding the timing of the Ninth Step, the AA Big Book says,
"Now we go out to our fellows and repair the damage done in the
past."[1] Once your sponsee has completed the list of people he or
she has harmed and has declared his or her willingness to make
amends and to forgive, there is no reason to delay taking Step
Nine. Conceptually, Step Nine is the second half of Step Eight. It
translates our stated willingness to make amends into the action
of making them.

Step Study

The following readings and questions are suggested for your
sponsee as preparation for taking Step Nine. Answers to the
questions can be found in the readings, in "Understanding the
Ninth Step" later in this chapter, and in your sponsee's personal
experience.

Readings on the Step

1. Those pages in the AA Big Book that cover Step Nine (pages 76–84).
2. "Step Nine" in the AA Twelve and Twelve (pages 83–87).
3. Other readings on the Step appropriate to your particular Twelve Step program: _____

_____

4. _____

_____

Questions about the Step

1. What does the phrase "direct amends" mean?
2. What does the phrase "wherever possible" mean?
3. What does the word "reparations" mean?
4. What does the phrase "except when to do so would injure them or others" mean?
5. What guidelines will you follow in determining the amend to be made to each person?
6. Are you willing to suffer whatever consequences are necessary for you to properly take this Step?

Activities for the Step

Add a sixth column to your amends list from Step Eight and entitle it "Amends." In this column, describe the amend you intend to make to each person on the list.

Understanding the Ninth Step

Bill Wilson writes, "Good judgment, a careful sense of timing, courage, and prudence—these are the qualities we shall need when we take Step Nine."[2] It is a painful, humbling Step. But it is also rewarding. AA's Twelve Promises are said to come true with the Ninth Step. These promises will also come true for members of other Twelve Step Fellowships who work this Step.

Step Nine calls for two sets of actions. In order to work this Step, we

1. Determine, after prayer and consultation with our sponsor, the specific amends we need to make to each person we have harmed. What must we do in order to repair, to the best of our ability, the damage we have done?
2. Make the actual amends to each person on our Eighth Step list.

> *In Step Nine, we determine the exact amends*
> *we need to make. Then we make them.*

Of Step Nine, the AA Big Book says, "We attempt to sweep away the debris which has accumulated out of our effort to live on self-will and run the show ourselves."[3] Our new beginning is based on a new set of principles—on God's will for us rather than on our own.

Key concepts

THE NATURE OF AMENDS

Step Nine focuses on the specific amends we need to make for the injuries we have caused others in the past. Another word for amends is "reparation." It means an action taken to repair something. A reparation provides some form of compensation or repayment to a person who has suffered a loss or injury as a result of our actions. Reparation is an appropriate word for what we are trying to do. It is not enough just to apologize if anything more can be done.

The AA Big Book says, "Although these reparations take innumerable forms, there are some general principles which we find guiding. Reminding ourselves that we have decided to go to any lengths to find a spiritual experience, we ask that we be given strength and direction to do the right thing, no matter what the

personal consequences may be. We may lose our position or reputation or face jail, but we are willing. We have to be. We must not
shrink at anything."[4]

> *To make a reparation is to repair the damage.*
> *It is more than an apology.*

We need to be willing to do whatever it takes to make things right,
even if it involves great personal sacrifice and dire consequences, as
long as it does not injure someone else. The AA Big Book is clear
on the necessity of this commitment. In today's society in which it
is so often acceptable to blame others rather than to accept the consequences of our own behavior, the actions called for in this Step
may seem harsh. Most of us want to escape the fear and suffering
that Step Nine creates. We hope to avoid making painful amends by
pleading some reason for the harm we've caused other than our
own character defects. Or we look for some excuse to avoid the
consequences. But there is no "easier, softer way" that works.

> *Some amends may mean great personal sacrifice.*
> *We make them anyway.*

MAKING DIRECT AMENDS

Step Nine uses the term "direct amends" to emphasize that the
amends—the reparations—must be made directly to the person
harmed "wherever possible." The power of the Step lies in facing
the *person* we have wronged as well as in confronting the wrongs
themselves and in trying to correct them. The pain of this Step
and the ego-deflation it brings come directly from this confrontation. We cannot, therefore, make an "indirect" amend by, for
example, giving money to a charity *as long as a direct amend is
possible and appropriate.*

> *The power of Step Nine lies in making the amend*
> *directly to the person harmed.*

But when is a direct amend appropriate? Whenever it can be made without injuring another person, whether it is the person harmed or an innocent third party. In choosing *not* to make a direct amend, our only reason must be that it would result in harm to another person. As the AA Twelve and Twelve says, "The only exceptions we will make will be cases where our disclosure would cause actual harm."[5] Bill Wilson writes, "We cannot buy our own peace of mind at the expense of others."[6] On the other hand, we cannot avoid an amend just because it would result in pain, suffering, or any other negative consequence to ourselves alone. "For the readiness to take the full consequences of our past acts, and to take responsibility for the well-being of others at the same time, is the very spirit of Step Nine."[7]

The only reason for not making a direct amend
is that it would injure someone else.

Some amends are straightforward. If we skipped out on our debts, we repay them. If we stole money, we repay that, too, even if we have to borrow the funds to do it. If we damaged a car, we repair it. If we ruined somebody's reputation by telling lies, we go to those whom we told the lies to and tell the truth even if it ruins our own reputation. It is better to build a new reputation than to drink or use again. If we caused anguish, then we ask ourselves how we can best make reparations for it. Whatever we did, we make reparations as long as it does not harm another person.

"There may be some wrongs we can never fully right," says the AA Big Book. "We don't worry about them if we can honestly say to ourselves that we would right them if we could."[8] Even in these cases, however, we try to repair the damage, however indirect or incomplete the reparation may be. Some kind of action is required. Even if the person we harmed is dead, we can do something to make amends for the injury we caused.

Some kind of amend is required
even if we can't completely repair the damage.

The determination of whether or not to make a direct amend is made in consultation with our sponsor. The AA Twelve and Twelve describes four potential classes of amends: "There will be those who ought to be dealt with just as soon as we become reasonably confident that we can maintain our sobriety. There will be those to whom we can make only partial restitution, lest complete disclosures do them or others more harm than good. There will be other cases where action ought to be deferred, and still others in which by the very nature of the situation we shall never be able to make direct personal contact at all."[9]

Amends related to adultery, crimes, or acts that might result in being fired from a job have the potential to harm others. They should be thoroughly considered. Since these amends could involve injuring innocent third parties, the exact nature of the amend may not be clear without prayerful thought. Many a newcomer has charged into the Ninth Step without adequate guidance and has ended up causing further injury, much to his or her later regret. Some form of appropriate reparation can be developed, however, if the willingness is there.

> *The nature of each amend, including whether or*
> *not it should be direct, is determined through*
> *sponsee/sponsor consultation and prayer.*

OUR SIDE OF THE STREET

In making amends, it is easy to want to blame the other person rather than face our own character defects. We can't blame others and live within the spirit of the Ninth Step. We are concerned only with our side of the street, not their side of the street. Regardless of what they have done, we hold ourselves accountable for our contribution to the problem. Otherwise, we cannot be free.

The AA Big Book describes how to make amends to someone we dislike or whom we would prefer to blame for our troubles. It states, "We go to him in a helpful and forgiving spirit, confessing our former ill feeling and expressing our regret. "Under no circumstances do we criticize such a person or argue. . . . We are there to sweep off our side of the street, realizing that nothing worthwhile can be accomplished until we do so, never trying to tell him what he should do. His faults are not discussed. We stick to our own."[10]

*In making an amend, we are concerned
only with our side of the street.*

The purpose of working the Ninth Step is to right what we have done wrong. It makes no difference whether or not the injured party accepts our amend and our apology (although it's more pleasant when they do). It doesn't matter how they react insofar as this Step is concerned. Nor do they have to forgive us for us to be forgiven. Our forgiveness does not depend upon them. All we can do is the right thing. How they react to our effort is a matter between them and their Higher Power.

BECOMING WILLING

"If we haven't the will to do this [Step], we ask until it comes," according to the AA Big Book.[11] We pray daily for the strength and courage to do what we have to do in Step Nine. Although we became willing to make amends in Step Eight, that willingness sometimes needs a boost in Step Nine. Prayer is the booster.

*When our resolve to do this Step weakens,
we pray for willingness.*

Applying Step Nine

Since the Ninth Step is worked only in connection with Step Eight, it is possible that Step Nine will be worked only once. If the wreckage of the past has been dealt with completely the first time, it isn't necessary to do it again.

Sponsor Guidelines for Working Step Nine

Suggest that your sponsee do the readings and answer the questions listed under "Step Study." When your sponsee has completed this work, ask him or her to make an appointment with you to discuss the Step.

First meeting on the Step

Based on the suggested readings, "Understanding the Ninth Step" in this chapter, and your own knowledge and experience, discuss Step Nine with your sponsee. You may want to use the study questions or "Understanding the Step" as a discussion guide.

Second meeting on the Step

In the second meeting, discuss the amends your sponsee intends to make. If difficult decisions have to be made involving adultery, theft, or other activities that involve innocent third parties, discuss them in detail. Consider the guidelines in the basic text of your Fellowship and the Twelve and Twelve or equivalent. Remember the need for your sponsee to be willing to do whatever is necessary regardless of the possible consequences to himself or herself alone.

Assist your sponsee in avoiding the "easier, softer way" that will undermine the purpose of the Step and shortchange him or her in the long run. For example, your sponsee may not want to make the financial sacrifices necessary to repay a debt, replace something stolen, or otherwise pay for reparations that need to be made. If so, remind him or her that the Step often requires serious sacrifices if it is to be worked properly and the AA Promises are to be fulfilled. The essence of the Step is facing the consequences of our character defects and making right the wrongs we have committed to the best of our abilities to do so. If those consequences now involve financial sacrifices, we have to make them.

Help your sponsee avoid the temptation
of incomplete amends. They aren't enough.

The final decision on what amends to make is your sponsee's. If you disagree with that decision, however, explain why, including what you think the results of his or her actions might be. Urge your sponsee to pray about difficult amends and to listen to his or her intuition. In the case of complex decisions, continue to pray until the right answer comes. It will always come.

When you and your sponsee agree on the amends to be made to each person on the list, it is time for your sponsee to make the amends. Monitor his or her progress as he or she goes about this task. If your sponsee is undecided about one or two of the amends to be made, he or she can still get started on the others right away.

When sponsees procrastinate on this Step, it means that they have not yet worked Step Eight. Until the willingness to make amends is there from Step Eight, Step Nine is impossible. When sponsees resist this Step, take them back to Steps Eight and Three. Why are they unwilling to turn their will and their lives over to the care of God in this area of amends (Step Three)? They should also consider whether or not they are still willing to have their defects of character removed (Step Six) and whether or not they want a restoration to sanity (Step Two). Of Steps Eight and Nine, the AA Big Book reminds us, "Remember it was agreed at the beginning *we would go to any lengths for victory over alcohol.*"[12] For members of the other Twelve Step Fellowships, the same commitment is necessary for victory over drugs or compulsive behavior.

When your sponsee delays this Step,
take him or her back to Steps Two, Three, Six,
and Eight for more work.

Sponsee questions

Sponsees often have questions about Step Nine. Here are some of the common questions.

> *What if I cheated on my spouse and*
> *he or she doesn't know about it?*
> *Do I have to make a direct amend?*

Questions like these have to be answered sponsee by sponsee. The guiding principle, however, is not to do something that would harm the person receiving the amend or innocent third parties. Bill Wilson wrote that we don't have the right to achieve peace of mind through a confession that harms someone else.[13] If such a confession would hurt your spouse or children, it should probably not be made. The amend that gets made in this case may not involve an admission of the affair but rather an apology made in prayer and a new set of behaviors aimed at setting things right in the future.

> *What if I could get in trouble*
> *for this or even go to jail for this?*

The same principle applies as in the first question. The issue is whether or not an innocent third party will be harmed if you "get in trouble" or go to jail. For example, if going to jail will mean the end of a paycheck that will reduce your spouse and children to poverty, there may be a better way than a direct amend in the form of a confession. Some kind of amend, however, has to be made, perhaps in the form of long-term community service. If, the reparation is repayment of stolen funds, the money may have to be repaid anonymously. Questions like these should be thoroughly discussed with your sponsor.

> *I stole/borrowed a lot more money*
> *than I make now. It will take me years*
> *to pay it back. Do I have to do that?*

The guidelines suggest that you should make reparations, meaning amends that repair the damage your behavior caused. Whether or not it will mean financial sacrifice for you is not a consideration. How it will affect your family, on the other hand, may be. But your family cannot serve as an excuse for you not to pay the consequences for your past inappropriate behavior. It may be that you will have to work out a long repayment schedule. Work with your sponsor to determine the exact amend to be made.

Taking Step Nine

The last meeting on Step Nine occurs when your sponsee reports that he or she has made all the amends. Ask your sponsee if he or she

- Has made the best and most complete reparation possible to everyone on the list.
- Has any nagging doubts about a person or an amend.
- Is satisfied that the Step has been taken.

Since AA's Twelve Promises are said to come true with the Ninth Step, ask your sponsee to read them if AA is your Fellowship. They appear in the last paragraph on page 83 of the AA Big Book and in the first two paragraphs on page 84 and in appendix B of this book (page 228). When your sponsee has finished reading the Promises, Step Nine has been taken.

If AA is not your Fellowship, congratulate your sponsee on the completion of a difficult Step and suggest that he or she move on to Step Ten.

18

Working Step Ten

*Continued to take personal inventory
and when we were wrong promptly admitted it.*

Timing of Step Ten

Once your sponsee has worked Step Nine, he or she is ready to begin Step Ten.

Step Study

The following readings and questions are suggested for your sponsee as preparation for taking Step Ten. Answers to the questions can be found in the readings, in "Understanding the Tenth Step" later in this chapter, and in your sponsee's personal experience.

Readings on the Step

1. Those pages in the AA Big Book that cover Step Ten (pages 84–85).
2. "Step Ten" in the AA Twelve and Twelve (pages 88–95).

3. Other readings on the Step appropriate to your particular Twelve Step program: ———————————————————————

———————————————————————————————————————

4. ———————————————————————————————————————

———————————————————————————————————————

Questions about the Step

1. Why does the Step begin with "Continued to take . . ."?
2. What does the phrase "personal inventory" mean as it is used in this Step?
3. Why is the process of taking an inventory as important as admitting when we are wrong?
4. What are the actions we are supposed to take each day in order to work the Tenth Step?
5. What does it mean to be "wrong," and what are some recent examples of "being wrong" from your own life?
6. What are your major character defects and how are they likely to show themselves in behavior that requires the application of this Step?
7. What does it mean to "promptly admit it" when we are wrong? Why is it important to *promptly* admit it?
8. Are you willing to make the commitment and the effort necessary to work this Step, one day at a time?
9. If you resist this Step, why do you think you are resisting it?
10. How will you know when you have taken this Step?

Understanding the Tenth Step

With Step Ten, the AA Big Book tells us, sanity has returned. "We will seldom be interested in liquor. If tempted, we recoil from it as from a hot flame. We react sanely and normally, and we will find that this has happened automatically."[1] The same return to sanity can be expected in other Twelve Step Fellowships with the Tenth Step.

The process of looking at our character defects and our wrongs that we began in the Fourth Step continues with this Step. "We have entered the world of the Spirit. Our next function is to grow in understanding and effectiveness."[2]

With the Tenth Step, sanity has returned.

Now that we have cleaned up the mistakes of the past and made reparations for them, this Step tells us how to maintain the new state of serenity and freedom we have achieved. With Step Ten, we monitor our character defects and their consequences through a daily inventory, taking prompt corrective action as needed to keep our slate clean and our character defects in check.

The Tenth Step is Steps Four through Nine in a single package applied to the present. Working Step Ten means adopting a way of life that requires continuous commitment and effort. The difficulties—and the rewards—of the Step come from applying it to our lives day after day, month after month, year after year. It is an essential part of the Twelve Steps' spiritual program and of what the AA Big Book calls its "design for living" that keeps the Twelve Promises coming true in our lives.

Step Ten is Steps Four through Nine applied daily.

Key concepts

TAKING INVENTORY

The personal inventory described in this Step is the same kind of inventory we took in Step Four. It is still a searching and fearless moral inventory that examines our character defects and our behavior. The AA Big Book and the Twelve and Twelve describe the way in which we are to work the Tenth Step:

· During the day, we take a spot-check inventory "whenever we find ourselves getting tangled up."[3]

- At the end of the day, we take a personal inventory to review the events of the hours just past.
- Our personal inventory at the end of the day is in the form of a balance sheet, which means that we include in the inventory what we have done *right* as well as what we have done wrong.
- Whenever selfishness, dishonesty, resentments, or fear crop up, "we ask God at once to remove them. We discuss them with someone immediately and make amends quickly if we have harmed anyone. Then we resolutely turn our thoughts to someone we can help."[4]
- We forgive when the fault is elsewhere.[5]
- "Love and tolerance of others is our code."[6]

The Tenth Step is a daily application
of the Golden Rule:
Treat others as we would like to be treated.

The AA Twelve and Twelve asks, "Aren't these practices joy-killers as well as time-consumers?"[7] The answer is no. "A continuous look at our assets and liabilities, and a real desire to learn and grow by this means, are necessities for us. . . . More experienced people, of course, in all times and places have practiced unsparing self-survey and criticism. For the wise have always known that no one can make much of his life until self-searching becomes a regular habit, until he is able to admit and accept what he finds, and until he patiently and persistently tries to correct what is wrong."[8]

The AA Twelve and Twelve suggests,
"When in doubt [about what to do],
we can always pause, saying,
'Not my will, but Thine, be done.' "[9]

ADMITTING IT WHEN WE ARE WRONG

It is hard for many of us to admit we are wrong. It is humbling. We prefer to be right. But we are wrong whenever we act out of our character defects, whenever we live in our self-centeredness, or whenever we harm others. For example, we are wrong when we blame other people rather than accept responsibility for what we have done, when we try to get away with something rather than own up to it, when we lie to protect ourselves or our image. We are wrong when we are judgmental, self-righteous, or demanding.

Step Ten asks us to *promptly* admit when we are wrong. A prompt admission is more effective than a delayed one in helping us acknowledge our negative behavior and to change it. A prompt admission is also more effective in defusing the anger that our inappropriate behavior has caused in others. The prompt admission we make is an amend, but the amend we need to make may also involve reparations, as with Step Nine. We may have to repair the damage we caused.

> **Step Ten requires us to**
> **promptly admit when we are wrong.**

Why are all these amends so important? Because Twelve Step programs are programs of spiritual development. Spiritual growth requires that we be honest about who we are and what we have done. It requires that we acknowledge our past behavior which has injured others, repair the damage that behavior caused, and then not behave that way again. An essential part of understanding the amends process is to recognize that a complete amend includes *not repeating the same behavior*. The amends and the apologies we made in the Ninth Step mean little if we do not change the way we behave. It is for this reason that Step Ten follows Step Nine. It keeps us from repeating the wrongs of the past.

> **Our amends are not complete**
> **unless we stop repeating the behavior**
> **that has harmed others in the past.**

Despite all the good effects of this Step, we resist it. Why? Part of the answer may be that we resist humility and the deflation of our egos that accompanies it. As the Twelve Step saying goes, we still "want what we want when we want it." We are still too often self-will run riot.

There is another concept connected with Step Ten that is often difficult for the newly recovering person to understand: "It is a spiritual axiom that every time we are disturbed, no matter what the cause, there is something wrong *with us*."[10] We are so used to blaming others for the way things are or the way we feel, that it seems strange, at first, to think that *we* might be the cause of our own unhappiness. How can *we* be the problem? The AA Twelve and Twelve names several causes of this self-disturbance: "justifiable" anger, resentments, jealousy, envy, self-pity, and hurt pride.[11] Only when we understand the source of our unhappiness, can we do something about it. "A spot-check inventory taken in the midst of such disturbances can be of very great help in quieting stormy emotions."[12] A quick phone call to our sponsor can help too.

> *Whenever we are disturbed,*
> *we can use a spot-check inventory*
> *to set things right.*

One of the most often quoted lines in the AA Big Book appears in the discussion on Step Ten: "We are not cured of alcoholism. What we really have is a daily reprieve contingent on the maintenance of our spiritual condition."[13] The same "daily reprieve" is part of recovery in other Twelve Step Fellowships as well. The Big Book says, "Every day is a day when we must carry the vision of God's will into all of our activities. 'How can I best serve Thee— Thy will (not mine) be done.' These are thoughts that must go with us constantly."[14] God's will for us as recovering people, most of us have determined, includes the removal of our character defects. An ongoing self-appraisal, a daily inventory, and the amends we need to make constitute the footwork we do toward the removal of our defects of character.

Applying the Step

Step Ten is applied daily. It is never "worked" in the past tense; it is always "being worked" in the present tense. In combination with the Eleventh Step, Step Ten is the primary mechanism for keeping our egos in check and our self-will restrained. Excuses to avoid working Step Ten come easily. The best defense against slacking off is self-discipline, prayer, and a sponsor who will help monitor our application of this Step.

Step Ten is a combination of taking an inventory regularly and promptly admitting when we are wrong. Some of us are tempted to ignore the inventory part and concentrate on admitting it when we are wrong. But the Step consists of both parts. We are not working the Tenth Step unless we are doing both.

We learn to work Step Ten by working it over and over. A daily working of Step Ten is a habit to be developed, and habits are developed by repetition.

Sponsor Guidelines for Working Step Ten

Suggest that your sponsee do the readings and answer the questions listed under "Step Study." When your sponsee has completed this work, ask him or her to make an appointment with you to discuss the Step.

First meeting on the Step

Based on the suggested readings, "Understanding the Tenth Step" in this chapter, and your own knowledge and experience, discuss Step Ten with your sponsee. You may want to use the study questions or "Understanding the Tenth Step" as a discussion guide.

Taking Step Ten

An important question to resolve with your sponsee is how to determine when the Step has been taken for purposes of moving on to Step Eleven. Since the Tenth Step process continues for a lifetime, there is no definitive answer. A good guideline, however, is that the Step has been taken when your sponsee has worked the Step long enough to have developed a regular habit of self-examination and has gained enough humility and willingness to promptly admit his or her wrongs. On that basis, three criteria can be used to determine whether or not your sponsee has taken Step Ten. They are as follows:

1. Is there a continuing commitment to put forth the effort that the Step requires?
2. Is there evidence of the Step's daily application in your sponsee's life? Has he or she developed a habit of spot-check inventories and end-of-the-day inventories? When wrong, does he or she promptly admit it?
3. Does your sponsee have a sense of God-consciousness? Has he or she begun "to develop this vital sixth sense" as the AA Big Book puts it?[15]

When all three criteria have been met, your sponsee has taken Step Ten and is ready to begin Step Eleven with the reminder that the Tenth Step is never completed.

19

Working
Step Eleven

Sought through prayer and meditation to improve
our conscious contact with God as we understood Him,
praying only for knowledge of His will for us
and the power to carry that out.

Timing of Step Eleven

At the end of the discussion on Step Ten, the AA Big Book says, "But we must go further and that means more action." Your sponsee can begin Step Eleven as soon as the Tenth Step has been taken and is being worked daily.

Step Study

The following readings and questions are suggested for your sponsee as preparation for taking Step Eleven. Answers to the questions can be found in the readings, in "Understanding the Eleventh Step" later in this chapter, and in your sponsee's personal experience.

Readings on the Step

1. Those pages in the AA Big Book that cover Step Eleven (pages 85–88).

2. "Step Eleven" in the AA Twelve and Twelve (pages 96–105).
3. Other readings on the Step appropriate to your particular Twelve Step program: _____

_____

4. _____

_____

Questions about the Step

1. What is prayer?
2. What is meditation?
3. How often do you pray and meditate?
4. What would it mean for you to improve your conscious contact with God?
5. What is your understanding of God?
6. Why pray *only* for knowledge of God's will?
7. Why pray for the power to carry out God's will?

Understanding the Eleventh Step

Our sobriety depends on the maintenance of our spiritual condition. The powerlessness over our addictions or compulsions that nearly destroyed us will return if we do not work on maintaining our contact with a Higher Power. In Step Eleven, we carry that goal further: we seek to *improve* the conscious contact with God that we have established in the previous Steps.

Key concepts

PRAYER AND MEDITATION

"Prayer and meditation are our principal means of conscious contact with God,"[1] says the AA Twelve and Twelve. Bill Wilson writes, "There is a direct linkage among self-examination, meditation, and prayer. Taken separately, these practices can bring much relief and benefit. But when they are logically related and interwoven, the result is an unshakable foundation for life."[2]

Both the AA Big Book and the Twelve and Twelve refer to the benefits of prayer. "Almost the only scoffers at prayer are those who never tried it enough," quotes the Twelve and Twelve. ". . . We have found that the actual good results of prayer are beyond question. They are matters of knowledge and experience. All those who have persisted have found strength not ordinarily their own. They have found wisdom beyond their usual capacity. And they have increasingly found a peace of mind which can stand firm in the face of difficult circumstances."[3]

> *Our experience in Twelve Step recovery*
> *is that prayer and meditation work.*

It is through prayer and meditation that we reestablish our desire to do God's will. A handy distinction that program members often make between prayer and meditation is this: prayer is speaking to God, whereas meditation is listening to God. We need to ask God to reveal His will to us, but we must also listen in order to hear the answer.

Part of all prayer and meditation is self-examination. Bill Wilson writes, "As we have seen, self-searching is the means by which we bring new vision, action, and grace to bear upon the dark and negative side of our natures. It is a step in the development of that kind of humility that makes it possible for us to receive God's help."[4] We must continually work on the character defects that stand between us and serenity, between what we are and what God's will for us is.

> *Self-examination is a goal*
> *of prayer and meditation.*

The program of prayer and meditation that the AA Big Book lays out in Step Eleven is rigorous. It is certainly a departure from the routine of our drinking, using, or compulsive days and even of our early recovery. Many of us will resist prayer and meditation.

We tend to be a rebellious lot, and the idea of a daily effort to find humility is not necessarily appealing. We may still want our own way. We may still think we are "too busy" to take time out for prayer and meditation. Why do we resist submitting to our Higher Power even when we have convincing evidence that such submission is the only way to real power? The answer seems to lie in self-will run riot.

Bill Wilson wrote that when we aren't doing well, "the chances are better than even that we shall locate our trouble in our mis-understanding or neglect of A.A.'s Step Eleven—prayer, medi-tation, and the guidance of God."[5] He continues, "The other Steps can keep most of us sober and somehow functioning. But Step Eleven can keep us growing, if we try hard and work at it continually."[6]

> *The Eleventh Step calls for a rigorous program*
> *of prayer and meditation.*

MORNING PRAYER AND MEDITATION

Upon awakening, the AA Big Book suggests that we "think about the twenty-four hours ahead. We consider our plans for the day. Before we begin, we ask God to direct our thinking, especially asking that it be divorced from self-pity, dishonest or self-seeking motives."[7] As we think about the forthcoming day, we ask God to help us determine the proper course of action when we face inde-cision. "We ask God for inspiration, an intuitive thought or a decision. We relax and take it easy. We don't struggle. We are often surprised how the right answers come after we have tried this for a while. What used to be the hunch or the occasional inspiration gradually becomes a working part of the mind."[8]

Some Twelve Step program members use meditation books with appropriate themes and quotations. *Twenty-Four Hours a Day* is the AA classic. Others meditate on portions of the AA Big Book or its equivalent, the Twelve and Twelve, or other Twelve Step literature. Favorite meditation selections in the AA Big Book include the Third Step Prayer (page 63), the Seventh Step Prayer (page 76), the Promises (pages 83–84), "A Vision for You" (page 164), or a specific Step. Whatever the piece of literature, its purpose is to help us feel the presence of God as we understand God and to sense God's direction for our lives.

We conclude our period of morning meditation "with a prayer that we be shown all through the day what our next step is to be, that we be given whatever we need to take care of such problems. We ask especially for freedom from self-will. . . . We are careful never to pray for our own selfish ends."[9]

"Dr. Bob's morning devotion consisted of a short prayer, a twenty-minute study of a familiar verse from the Bible, and a quiet period of waiting for directions as to where he, that day, should find use for his talent. Having heard, he would religiously go about his Father's business, as he put it."[10] Bill Wilson and his wife continued their morning meditation together until his death in 1971. Bill said, "I sort of always felt that something was lost from A.A. when we stopped emphasizing the morning meditation."[11]

Step Nine calls for daily morning prayer and meditation.

DAYTIME PRAYER AND MEDITATION

The AA Big Book suggests, "As we go through the day we pause, when agitated or doubtful, and ask for the right thought or action. We constantly remind ourselves we are no longer running the show, humbly saying to ourselves many times each day, 'Thy will be done.' We are then in much less danger of excitement, fear, anger, worry, self-pity, or foolish decisions."[12]

The AA Twelve and Twelve reminds us that "meditation is in reality intensely practical. One of its first fruits is emotional balance."[13]

We can use prayer and meditation during the day to regain a sense of emotional balance.

EVENING PRAYER AND MEDITATION

Upon retiring, the AA Big Book says, "we constructively review our day. Were we resentful, selfish, dishonest or afraid? Do we owe an apology? Have we kept something to ourselves which should be discussed with another person at once? Were we kind and loving toward all? What could we have done better? Were we thinking of ourselves most of the time? Or were we thinking of what we could do for others, of what we could pack into the stream of life?"[14]

After taking this inventory of our behavior and the ways in which our character defects manifested themselves, "we ask God's forgiveness and inquire what corrective measures should be taken."[15] What lessons has the day presented that we can use in changing our future behavior? How has our will been in line with God's and how has it clashed? These are the questions we ask ourselves.

In the evening, we inventory
our behavior for the day.

WHAT TO PRAY FOR

With Step Eleven, we complete the process of ego-deflation that we began in the First Step by praying *only* for knowledge of God's will for us and the power to carry that out. We act upon the decision we made in the Third Step more fully. Of course, we cannot work Step Eleven perfectly, and so our ego-deflation is not complete. But we have, over the course of working eleven Steps, developed a true spiritual basis for living. That basis is humility: putting God's will before our own.

With regard to how to pray, Dr. Samuel Shoemaker, Bill Wilson's spiritual advisor, said that a person must "grow up and stop just *using* God and begin to ask God to *use him [or her]*." According to this Episcopal priest (in words from the 1950s), "Real prayer is not telling God what *we* want. It is putting ourselves at His disposal so that He can tell us what He wants. Prayer is not trying to get God to change His will. It is trying to find out what His will is, to align ourselves or realign ourselves with His purpose for the world and for us."[16] Hence, the Step suggests that we pray only for the knowledge of God's will for us and the power to carry it out. Bill Wilson suggested that "when making specific requests, it will be well to add to each one of them this qualification: '. . . if it be Thy will.'"[17]

Regardless of what we may want,
our prayer is that God's will be done.

Applying Step Eleven

Step Eleven has multiple daily applications: upon awakening in the morning and upon retiring at night, and whenever we face indecision or feel agitated during the day. The AA Big Book is specific about how the Step is to be applied. Bill Wilson wrote, "It would be easy to be vague about this matter [of prayer and meditation]. Yet, we believe we can make some definite and valuable suggestions."[18]

If we are not careful, we can fall into the trap of thinking that Step Eleven is being fulfilled if we only pray now and then or when we are in trouble. Such a reading of the Step is inaccurate. Step Eleven lays out a rigorous program of prayer and meditation that we are to follow daily. It requires serious self-discipline to work this Step. We are kidding ourselves if we think that Step Eleven "comes naturally" to most of us or is a Step to be worked infrequently.

Without living the regular program of prayer, meditation, and self-examination described in Step Eleven, we are not working this Step. Our performance with Step Eleven may be very uneven over the years. Sometimes we are willing and sometimes we are not. Especially in the beginning, it may take a lot of effort to develop a habit of prayer and meditation. Once developed, however, the fruits of practicing Step Eleven create a momentum that carries us forward. Even so, we will occasionally fall back into our old ways. Such regressions are one of the reasons we need sponsors who can remind us when we are not working this Step.

**Working part of Step Eleven
is not the same as working Step Eleven.**

Sponsor Guidelines for Step Eleven

Suggest that your sponsee do the readings and answer the questions listed under "Step Study." When your sponsee has completed this work, ask him or her to make an appointment with you to discuss the Step.

First meeting on the Step

Based on the suggested readings, "Understanding the Eleventh Step" in this chapter, and your own knowledge and experience, discuss Step Eleven with your sponsee. You may want to use the study questions or "Understanding the Step" as a discussion guide. In particular, outline the rigorous schedule of prayer and meditation that the Eleventh Step suggests.

A question that is often asked by sponsees is, "When has Step Eleven been 'worked'?" The answer is that it has never *been worked*. Since the Eleventh Step is a daily process that continues for a lifetime, it can only *be worked*. When your sponsee has worked the Step long enough to develop a habit of daily prayer, meditation, and self-examination and has a well-developed sense of "conscious contact" with his or her Higher Power, the Step is being worked. For purposes of moving on to Step Twelve, it also can be considered to have been taken.

Taking Step Eleven

Three criteria can be used to determine whether or not your sponsee is working Step Eleven and is ready to move on to Step Twelve. They are

1. Is your sponsee seeking to improve his or her "conscious contact" with God by following a regular program of daily prayer and meditation in the morning, during the day, and in the evening?
2. Does your sponsee pray *only* for knowledge of God's will for him or her and for the power to carry it out?
3. Has your sponsee been working the Step in this manner long enough to have a continuing commitment?

When these criteria are being met, your sponsee has taken the Step.

20

Working
Step Twelve

Having had a spiritual awakening
as the result of these steps,
we tried to carry this message to alcoholics,
and to practice these principles in all our affairs.

Timing of Step Twelve

At the end of the discussion on Step Eleven, the AA Big Book says, "But this is not all. There is action and more action. 'Faith without works is dead.' "[1]

Your sponsee can begin Step Twelve as soon as he or she has taken Step Eleven.

Step Study

The following readings and questions are suggested for your sponsee as preparation for taking Step Twelve. Answers to the questions can be found in the readings, in "Understanding the Twelfth Step" later in this chapter, and in your sponsee's personal experience.

Readings on the Step

1. Those pages in the AA Big Book that cover Step Twelve (pages 89–103).
2. Appendix 2 ("Spiritual Experience") in the AA Big Book (Pages 569–570).
3. "Step Twelve" in the AA Twelve and Twelve (pages 106–125).
4. Other readings on the Step appropriate to your particular Twelve Step program: _____

_____

5. _____

_____

Questions about the Step

1. What does the term "spiritual awakening" mean to you?
2. Have you had a spiritual awakening? How are you different spiritually from the way you were when you came into the program?
3. Why does the Step say that a spiritual awakening comes about "as the result of working these Steps" rather than as "a result of working these Steps"?
4. What is the message we are trying to carry to others suffering from alcoholism, addiction, or compulsive behaviors?
5. Why is it important that we carry this message?
6. What Twelfth Step work have you done in the past week? two weeks? four weeks?
7. What are the principles that we are to practice in all our affairs?

Understanding the Twelfth Step

The Twelfth Step sums up our Twelve Step recovery program as a lifetime undertaking based on the practice of spiritual principles and service to others with the same addiction or compulsion. Bill Wilson writes, "The joy of living is the theme of A.A.'s Twelfth

Step, and action is its key word. . . . Here we begin to practice all Twelve Steps of the program in our daily lives so that we and those about us may find emotional sobriety."[2] The transforming power of the Twelve Steps is now focused on the whole of life, and the recovering alcoholic or addict moves to a larger, more encompassing dimension: the world of the spirit.

It should not be surprising that someone
who thoroughly follows the path of the Twelve Steps
has a wonderful life.

An entire chapter of the AA Big Book (chapter 7: "Working with Others") is devoted to Step Twelve. The AA Big Book discussion of this Step can be divided into three parts:

· The spiritual awakening that results from working the Twelve Steps and the significance of that awakening.
· Working with other alcoholics, addicts, or compulsive people (carrying the message of Twelve Step recovery to others like ourselves both in and out of recovery).
· Dedication to a way of life that involves the practice of spiritual principles in all our affairs.

Key concepts

SPIRITUAL AWAKENING

Bill Wilson writes, "Practicing these Steps, we had a spiritual awakening about which finally there was no question."[3] Program members who work all Twelve Steps do undergo a spiritual awakening. There is no doubt about it. That's how the program works. But what exactly is a spiritual awakening? "Maybe there are as many definitions of spiritual awakening as there are people who have had them," Bill Wilson wrote. Fundamentally, though, a spiritual awakening can be thought of as "a new state of consciousness and being,"[4] as a "personality change sufficient to bring about recovery from alcoholism,"[5] or another addiction or

compulsion, and as an "awareness of a Power greater than ourselves."[6] The Big Book speaks of a transformation stemming from
access to a source of strength—a Power—which before we had
denied ourselves.

The results of a spiritual awakening are dramatic, although
they may take place over a long period of time. They include
changed perceptions, attitudes, and behavior. In fact, the difference between a spiritual awakening (which Dr. Bob had) and a
spiritual experience (which Bill Wilson had) is just a matter of
timing. The *experience* occurs suddenly and completely and, in
that brief period of time, is transformative. The *awakening* takes
much longer. The end result is substantially the same. Bill Wilson
had a spiritual experience and never drank again. Dr. Bob never
drank again and had a spiritual awakening.

> *We had a spiritual awakening*
> *as the result of these Steps.*

WORKING WITH OTHER ALCOHOLICS, ADDICTS, OR COMPULSIVE PEOPLE

The AA Big Book says, "Practical experience shows that nothing
will so much insure immunity from drinking as intensive work
with other alcoholics. It works when other activities fail."[7]

Alcoholics Anonymous was founded because Bill Wilson realized that he needed to work with another alcoholic in order to
stay sober. That realization led him to a meeting with Dr. Bob in
Akron, Ohio in 1935 and to AA's cofounding. This need to work
with other alcoholics is basic to the AA program and the reason
that the Fellowship was cofounded. It took two alcoholics to stay
sober, so it took two alcoholics to start AA.

Working with another alcoholic is called Twelfth Step work.
Since all the other Twelve Step Fellowships have evolved from AA,
they are all based on working with other individuals suffering
from the same addiction or compulsion. Twelfth Step work is as
central to each of them as it is to the AA Fellowship.

*Twelfth Step work means to carry the message of recovery
to other addicted or compulsive people like ourselves.*

Twelfth Step work in AA began the day after AA's official founding, before there even was a Twelfth Step. On June 11, 1935, the morning after Dr. Bob took his last drink, he told Bill Wilson that the two of them would be "much safer" if they "got active" working with other alcoholics.[8] Dr. Bob called a nurse he knew at City Hospital to find a drunk they could call on. Two days later, they met with Bill D. who got sober and became AA's third member.[9]

Speaking at AA's twentieth anniversary convention in St. Louis, Missouri, in 1955, Bill Wilson told the assembled members, "A.A.'s Twelfth Step, carrying the message, is the basic service that our fellowship gives; it is our principal aim and the main reason for our existence. A.A. is more than a set of principles; it is a society of recovered alcoholics in action. We *must* carry A.A.'s message; otherwise we ourselves may fall into decay and those who have not yet been given the truth may die. This is why we so often say that *action* is the magic word. Action to carry A.A.'s message is therefore the heart of our Third Legacy of Service."[10] The truth of these words also applies to other Twelve Step Fellowships.

*AA was founded because
Bill Wilson carried the message
of recovery to Dr. Bob.*

The AA Big Book spends a substantial portion of chapter 7 on how to work with other alcoholics, particularly those who are brand new to recovery. The suggestions it offers are based on the experience of Bill Wilson, Dr. Bob, and other AA pioneers. This chapter is still the most authoritative work on how to Twelve-Step someone. The paragraphs on "Twelve Stepping" are important to read. Times have changed in the last sixty years, but the basic principles have not.

*Twelfth Step work is one of the actions
we take in order to stay in recovery.*

"These principles" are the principles embodied in the Twelve Steps and supported by program tradition and slogans. Having learned to practice them in our dealings with other program members, we faced the big question that Bill Wilson posed: "What about the practice of these principles in *all* our affairs? Can we love the whole pattern of living as eagerly as we do the small segment of it we discover when we try to help other alcoholics achieve sobriety? . . . Can we actually carry the A.A. spirit into our daily work?"[11]

Whatever our addiction or compulsion, the challenge we meet in the Twelfth Step is to transfer our practice of the program's great principles into the whole of life. It is our call to honesty with self and others, to humility, to prayer and meditation, to self-examination, and to service. It means seeking to know the will of our Higher Power, acknowledging our character defects, admitting our mistakes and making amends for them, taking responsibility for that which we can change in life and accepting the things we cannot change. Practicing these principles, in the final analysis, is living life on life's terms. It is embracing reality.

In "Chapter Twelve" of the AA Twelve and Twelve, Bill Wilson describes the new life we can enjoy as recovering individuals working the Twelfth Step (in other words, all the Steps). It is a life characterized by remarkable transformation. From our days as "childish, emotionally sensitive, and grandiose"[12] people, we emerge as mature men and women with lives that are "useful and profoundly happy."[13]

Our grandiosity has been replaced by humility.

Applying Step Twelve

Step Twelve includes the principles of all the other Steps. It is to be applied daily in our lives. In fact, it becomes the *design* of our lives. Therefore, Step Twelve is never worked in the past tense. It is always being worked in the present tense, in the forever "now" of our lives.

Sponsor Guidelines for Working Step Twelve

Suggest that your sponsee do the readings and answer the questions listed under "Step Study." When your sponsee has completed this work, ask him or her to make an appointment with you to discuss the Step.

First meeting on the Step

Based on the suggested readings, "Understanding the Twelfth Step" in this chapter, and your own knowledge and experience, discuss Step Twelve with your sponsee. You may want to use the study questions or "Understanding the Twelfth Step" as a discussion guide.

Taking Step Twelve

Three criteria can be used to determine whether or not your sponsee has taken the Twelfth Step. They are

1. Has your sponsee had a spiritual awakening as the result of working the Twelve Steps? (If there has not been a spiritual awakening to some degree, there is a problem somewhere in the chain of Steps. Take your sponsee back through the Steps, one by one, until the problem Step is located.)
2. Is your sponsee carrying the message of recovery to other people who suffer from the same addiction or compulsion? In other words, is he or she going to meetings, making Twelve Step calls, doing service work?
3. Is your sponsee making a sincere and disciplined effort to practice the program's principles in all his or her affairs? The goal is progress, not perfection. But the effort must be there. You may wish to ask your sponsee for specific instances.

If all three criteria are being met, I believe that a sponsee has taken Step Twelve. The Step has not been finally worked, of course, until the end of a lifetime.

With the formal "completion" of Step Twelve, we enter a new phase of recovery. The compulsion is gone, whatever it was; a spiritual awakening has occurred; and the Twelve Promises are coming true in greater depth. Armed with a set of spiritual tools in the form of the Twelve Steps, we can now face and effectively handle the challenges of life that had once overwhelmed us. More than that, we can achieve serenity and enjoy a rich and rewarding life. The kind of person we had dreamed of being some day, we have at last become.

We have been restored to sanity.

In all this, we find the greatest of ironies. By admitting powerlessness, we have been given power; by surrendering, we have won. God has truly done for us what we could not do for ourselves. He has taken our greatest weakness and transformed it into our greatest strength in the Twelve Step Fellowship. He has taken our pain and suffering and turned them into healing for others. He has made it possible for us to be of service. He has given us meaning and direction, purpose and accomplishment. He has taken emptiness and filled it up. All these things, He has done though Twelve simple Steps worked with love, discipline, and courage— and a Power greater than ourselves.

21

Progress,
Not Perfection

Just as all the Steps except the First represent ideals rather than perfectly attainable goals, so the standards I have described in this book are ideals of sponsorship. All of us as sponsors and sponsees fall short. I certainly do. But that does not mean we should not have a picture of what the ideal might be so that we can continue to strive for it. "Progress, not perfection" doesn't mean we should not try. In fact, it means the opposite. We never give up trying just because we can't achieve perfection. On the other hand, we don't beat ourselves up for failing to achieve it either.

> **No one is a perfect sponsor.**
> **No one is a perfect sponsee.**
> **It's progress, not perfection, that counts.**

In the final analysis, what lies at the heart of the sponsorship process is the authenticity of the relationship we build with our sponsees. If we are honest and ethical with them, respect their vulnerability and their trust in us, help them work the Steps, and model Twelve Step principles to the best of our abilities, we will have served them well. And they will reward us many times over with their growth and development in the program, their insights into recovery, and the examples they have set for us. An AA friend of mine believes that "God loans us a sponsee for a time." We are to make the most of that loan, treasuring the time we have and the opportunity for the Twelfth Step work it provides.

Dr. Bob summed up the meaning of the Twelve Steps in two words, love and service.[1] That summary could apply to the meaning of sponsorship as well. We hold sponsees, like the proverbial bird, in the palm of our hand. If we squeeze our hand, we will keep the bird, but we will smother it. If we open our hand, we allow the bird to grow and live. But we also allow it the freedom to leave us and fly away. It is the act of helping sponsees grow enough in the program to leave us that is the true measure of our love and courage.

Another friend of mine once told me, "It's not just that we have to let people come into our lives. It's also that we have to let them leave." We are all on loan to each other. One way or another, nothing is permanent in life except the love that passed between us.

Appendices

AA Preamble*

Alcoholics Anonymous is a fellowship of men and women who share their experience, strength and hope with each other that they may solve their common problem and help others to recover from alcoholism.

The only requirement for membership is a desire to stop drinking. There are no dues or fees for A.A. membership; we are self-supporting through our own contributions. A.A. is not allied with any sect, denomination, politics, organization or institution; does not wish to engage in any controversy; neither endorses nor opposes any causes. Our primary purpose is to stay sober and help other alcoholics to achieve sobriety.

* The Preamble is based on a portion of the foreword to the first edition of the AA Big Book. It was first formulated by an *A.A. Grapevine* editor in 1946.[1]

AA's Twelve Promises*

If we are painstaking about this phase of our development, we will be amazed before we are half way through. We are going to know a new freedom and a new happiness. We will not regret the past nor wish to shut the door on it. We will comprehend the word serenity and we will know peace. No matter how far down the scale we have gone, we will see how our experience can benefit others. That feeling of uselessness and self-pity will disappear. We will lose interest in selfish things and gain interest in our fellows. Self-seeking will slip away. Our whole attitude and outlook upon life will change. Fear of people and of economic insecurity will leave us. We will intuitively know how to handle situations which used to baffle us. We will suddenly realize that God is doing for us what we could not do for ourselves.

Are these extravagant promises? We think not. They are being fulfilled among us—sometimes quickly, sometimes slowly. They will always materialize if we work for them.

---

* The Promises are taken from Chapter Six of the AA Big Book, pages 83–84. Reprinted with permission.

Twelve Steps of Alcoholics Anonymous*

1. We admitted we were powerless over alcohol—that our lives had become unmanageable.
2. Came to believe that a Power greater than ourselves could restore us to sanity.
3. Made a decision to turn our will and our lives over to the care of God *as we understood Him.*
4. Made a searching and fearless moral inventory of ourselves.
5. Admitted to God, to ourselves, and to another human being the exact nature of our wrongs.
6. Were entirely ready to have God remove all these defects of character.
7. Humbly asked Him to remove our shortcomings.
8. Made a list of all persons we had harmed, and became willing to make amends to them all.
9. Made direct amends to such people wherever possible, except when to do so would injure them or others.
10. Continued to take personal inventory and when we were wrong promptly admitted it.
11. Sought through prayer and meditation to improve our conscious contact with God *as we understood Him,* praying only for knowledge of His will for us and the power to carry that out.
12. Having had a spiritual awakening as the result of these steps, we tried to carry this message to alcoholics, and to practice these principles in all our affairs.

* The Twelve Steps of AA are taken from *Alcoholics Anonymous,* 3d ed., published by AA World Services, Inc., New York, N.Y., 59–60. Reprinted with permission of AA World Services, Inc. (See editor's note on copyright page.)

The Twelve Steps of Al-Anon*

1. We admitted we were powerless over alcohol—that our lives had become unmanageable.
2. Came to believe that a Power greater than ourselves could restore us to sanity.
3. Made a decision to turn our will and our lives over to the care of God *as we understood Him.*
4. Made a searching and fearless moral inventory of ourselves.
5. Admitted to God, to ourselves, and to another human being the exact nature of our wrongs.
6. Were entirely ready to have God remove all these defects of character.
7. Humbly asked Him to remove our shortcomings.
8. Made a list of all persons we had harmed, and became willing to make amends to them all.
9. Made direct amends to such people wherever possible, except when to do so would injure them or others.
10. Continued to take personal inventory and when we were wrong promptly admitted it.
11. Sought through prayer and meditation to improve our conscious contact with God *as we understood Him,* praying only for knowledge of His will for us and the power to carry that out.
12. Having had a spiritual awakening as the result of these steps, we tried to carry this message to others, and to practice these principles in all our affairs.

* Adapted from the Twelve Steps of Alcoholics Anonymous and reprinted with permission of AA World Services, Inc., New York, N.Y. The Twelve Steps of Al-Anon are taken from *Al-Anon Faces Alcoholism,* 2nd ed., published by Al-Anon Family Group Headquarters, Inc., New York, N.Y., 236–37. Reprinted with permission of Al-Anon Family Group, Inc., Virginia Beach, VA.

The Twelve Steps of Narcotics Anonymous*

1. We admitted that we were powerless over our addiction, that our lives had become unmanageable.
2. We came to believe that a Power greater than ourselves could restore us to sanity.
3. We made a decision to turn our will and our lives over to the care of God *as we understood Him.*
4. We made a searching and fearless moral inventory of ourselves.
5. We admitted to God, to ourselves, and to another human being the exact nature of our wrongs.
6. We were entirely ready to have God remove all these defects of character.
7. We humbly asked Him to remove our shortcomings.
8. We made a list of all persons we had harmed, and became willing to make amends to them all.
9. We made direct amends to such people wherever possible, except when to do so would injure them or others.
10. We continued to take personal inventory and when we were wrong promptly admitted it.
11. We sought through prayer and meditation to improve our conscious contact with God *as we understood Him,* praying only for knowledge of His will for us and the power to carry that out.
12. Having had a spiritual awakening as a result of these steps, we tried to carry this message to addicts, and to practice these principles in all our affairs.

The Twelve Steps of Overeaters Anonymous*

1. We admitted we were powerless over food—that our lives had become unmanageable.
2. Came to believe that a Power greater than ourselves could restore us to sanity.
3. Made a decision to turn our will and our lives over to the care of God *as we understood Him.*
4. Made a searching and fearless moral inventory of ourselves.
5. Admitted to God, to ourselves, and to another human being the exact nature of our wrongs.
6. Were entirely ready to have God remove all these defects of character.
7. Humbly asked Him to remove our shortcomings.
8. Made a list of all persons we had harmed, and became willing to make amends to them all.
9. Made direct amends to such people wherever possible, except when to do so would injure them or others.
10. Continued to take personal inventory and when we were wrong, promptly admitted it.
11. Sought through prayer and meditation to improve our conscious contact with God *as we understood Him,* praying only for knowledge of His will for us and the power to carry that out.
12. Having had a spiritual awakening as the result of these steps, we tried to carry this message to compulsive overeaters and to practice these principles in all our affairs.

---

* Adapted from the Twelve Steps of Alcoholics Anonymous and reprinted with permission of AA World Services, Inc. From *Overeaters Anonymous* ©1993 by Overeaters Anonymous, Inc., Rio Rancho, NM., p. 4.

*The Twelve Steps of Sex Addicts Anonymous**

1. We admitted we were powerless over our compulsive sexual behavior—that our lives had become unmanageable.
2. Came to believe that a Power greater than ourselves could restore us to sanity.
3. Made a decision to turn our will and our lives over to the care of God *as we understood God.*
4. Made a searching and fearless moral inventory of ourselves.
5. Admitted to God, to ourselves, and to another human being the exact nature of our wrongs.
6. Were entirely ready to have God remove all these defects of character.
7. Humbly asked God to remove our shortcomings.
8. Made a list of all persons we had harmed and became willing to make amends to them all.
9. Made direct amends to such people wherever possible, except when to do so would injure them or others.
10. Continued to take personal inventory and when we were wrong promptly admitted it.
11. Sought through prayer and meditation to improve our conscious contact with God *as we understood God,* praying only for knowledge of God's will for us and the power to carry that out.
12. Having had a spiritual awakening as the result of these Steps, we tried to carry this message to other sex addicts and to practice these principles in all our activities.

---

* The Twelve Steps of Sex Addicts Anonymous are adapted from the Twelve Steps of Alcoholics Anonymous and reprinted with permission of AA World Services, Inc., New York, N.Y.

The Twelve Steps of Gamblers Anonymous*

1. We admitted we were powerless over gambling—that our lives had become unmanageable.

2. Came to believe that a Power greater than ourselves could restore us to a normal way of thinking and living.

3. Made a decision to turn our will and our lives over to the care of this Power of our own understanding.

4. Made a searching and fearless moral and financial inventory of ourselves.

5. Admitted to ourselves and to another human being the exact nature of our wrongs.

6. Were entirely ready to have these defects of character removed.

7. Humbly asked God (of our understanding) to remove our shortcomings.

8. Made a list of all persons we had harmed and became willing to make amends to them all.

9. Made direct amends to such people wherever possible, except when to do so would injure them or others.

10. Continued to take personal inventory and when we were wrong, promptly admitted it.

11. Sought through prayer and meditation to improve our conscious contact with God *as we understand Him*, praying only for knowledge of His will for us and the power to carry that out.

12. Having made an effort to practice these principles in all our affairs, we tried to carry this message to other compulsive gamblers.

---

* The Twelve Steps of Gamblers Anonymous are adapted from the Twelve Steps of Alcoholics Anonymous. Reprinted with permission of AA World Services, Inc., New York, N.Y.

Twelve Traditions of Alcoholics Anonymous (Short Form)

1. Our common welfare should come first; personal recovery depends upon A.A. unity.
2. For our group purpose there is but one ultimate authority—a loving God as He may express Himself in our group conscience. Our leaders are but trusted servants; they do not govern.
3. The only requirement for A.A. membership is a desire to stop drinking.
4. Each group should be autonomous except in matters affecting other groups or A.A. as a whole.
5. Each group has but one primary purpose—to carry its message to the alcoholic who still suffers.
6. An A.A. group ought never endorse, finance, or lend the A.A. name to any related facility or outside enterprise, lest problems of money, property, and prestige divert us from our primary purpose.
7. Every A.A. group ought to be fully self-supporting, declining outside contributions.
8. Alcoholics Anonymous should remain forever nonprofessional, but our service centers may employ special workers.

---

* The Traditions were first published in the "long form" in the *A.A. Grapevine* of May 6, 1946, and were later confirmed at AA's First International Convention held in Cleveland, Ohio, in 1950. Bill Wilson wrote, "In reality I had not been the author of the Traditions at all. I had merely put them on paper in such a way as to mirror principles which had already been developed in A.A. group experience."[2]

Bill continued, "We saw that the A.A. Traditions were the key to the unity, the functioning, and even the survival of Alcoholics Anonymous.[3]...[They] are little else than a list of sacrifices which the experience of twenty years has taught us that we must make, individually and collectively, if A.A. itself is to stay alive and healthy."[4]

9. A.A., as such, ought never be organized; but we may create service boards or committees directly responsible to those they serve.

10. Alcoholics Anonymous has no opinion on outside issues; hence the A.A. name ought never be drawn into public controversy.

11. Our public relations policy is based on attraction rather than promotion; we need always maintain personal anonymity at the level of press, radio, and films.

12. Anonymity is the spiritual foundation of all our traditions, ever reminding us to place principles before personalities.

Endnotes

Chapter 1:
What Does a Sponsor Do?

1. *Living Sober* (New York: Alcoholics Anonymous World Services, Inc., 1975), 26.
2. *Questions and Answers on Sponsorship* (New York: Alcoholics Anonymous World Services, Inc.), 7.
3. *Twelve Steps and Twelve Traditions* (New York: Alcoholics Anonymous World Services, Inc., 1952), 117.

Chapter 3:
Some Questions Sponsees Ask about Sponsorship

1. *Lois Remembers* (New York: Al-Anon Family Group Headquarters, Inc., 1979), 87.
2. *'Pass It On,' The Story of Bill Wilson and How the A.A. Message Reached the World* (New York: Alcoholics Anonymous World Services, Inc., 1984), 242.

Chapter 4:
Some Questions Sponsees Ask about Their Sponsors

1. *Twelve Steps and Twelve Traditions* (New York: Alcoholics Anonymous World Services, Inc., 1952), 61.

Chapter 7:
Some Questions Sponsors Ask about Their Sponsees

1. *Alcoholics Anonymous Comes of Age: A Brief History of A.A.* (New York: Alcoholics Anonymous World Services, Inc., 1957), 244–45.
2. *Alcoholics Anonymous*, 3d ed. (New York: Alcoholics Anonymous World Services, Inc., 1976), 74.

3. *'Pass It On,'* *The Story of Bill Wilson and How the A.A. Message Reached the World* (New York: Alcoholics Anonymous World Services, Inc., 1984), 295.
4. *Three Talks to Medical Societies by Bill W., Co-founder of A. A.* (New York: Alcoholics Anonymous World Services, Inc.), 21.

Chapter 8:
Introducing the Steps

1. *Twelve Steps and Twelve Traditions* (New York: Alcoholics Anonymous World Services, Inc., 1952), 15.
2. *Dr. Bob and the Good Oldtimers: A Biography, with Recollections of Early A.A. in the Midwest* (New York: Alcoholics Anonymous World Services, Inc., 1980), 77.
3. *Alcoholics Anonymous,* 3d ed. (New York: Alcoholics Anonymous World Services, Inc., 1976), 58.
4. *Alcoholics Anonymous,* xiii.
5. *Alcoholics Anonymous Comes of Age: A Brief History of A.A.* (New York: Alcoholics Anonymous World Services, Inc., 1957), 159.
6. *Alcoholics Anonymous Comes of Age,* 160–61.
7. *Alcoholics Anonymous Comes of Age,* 161
8. Bill Wilson wrote only chapters 1–11 of the Big Book. Each of the personal stories were contributed by a different AA member who recounted his or her experience, strength, and hope about recovery in AA.
9. *Twelve Steps and Twelve Traditions,* 15.
10. *Twelve Steps and Twelve Traditions,* 17.
11. *Twelve Steps and Twelve Traditions,* 26.
12. *Twelve Steps and Twelve Traditions,* 40.
13. *Dr. Bob and the Good Oldtimers,* 101.
14. *Dr. Bob and the Good Oldtimers,* 102.
15. *Twelve Steps and Twelve Traditions,* 84.

Chapter 9:
Working Step One

1. *Twelve Steps and Twelve Traditions* (New York: Alcoholics Anonymous World Services, Inc., 1952), 68.
2. *Alcoholics Anonymous,* 3d ed. (New York: Alcoholics Anonymous World Services, Inc., 1976), 30.
3. *Alcoholics Anonymous,* 30.
4. *Twelve Steps and Twelve Traditions,* 24.
5. *Alcoholics Anonymous,* 30.
6. *Alcoholics Anonymous,* 31. Also, *Twelve Steps and Twelve Traditions,* 23.

Chapter 10:
Working Step Two

1. *Alcoholics Anonymous*, 3d ed. (New York: Alcoholics Anonymous World Services, Inc., 1976), 45.
2. *Alcoholics Anonymous*, 45.
3. *Twelve Steps and Twelve Traditions* (New York: Alcoholics Anonymous World Services, Inc., 1952), 27.
4. *Alcoholics Anonymous*, 47.
5. *Alcoholics Anonymous*, 46.
6. *Alcoholics Anonymous*, 44.
7. *Alcoholics Anonymous*, 60.

Chapter 11:
Working Step Three

1. *Alcoholics Anonymous*, 3d ed. (New York: Alcoholics Anonymous World Services, Inc., 1976), 60.
2. *Twelve Steps and Twelve Traditions* (New York: Alcoholics Anonymous World Services, Inc., 1952), 34.
3. *Twelve Steps and Twelve Traditions*, 40.
4. *Alcoholics Anonymous*, 47.
5. *Alcoholics Anonymous*, 62.
6. *Alcoholics Anonymous*, 62.
7. *Twelve Steps and Twelve Traditions*, 37–38.
8. *Alcoholics Anonymous*, 62.
9. *Alcoholics Anonymous*, 60.
10. *Twelve Steps and Twelve Traditions*, 35.
11. *Twelve Steps and Twelve Traditions*, 41.
12. *Alcoholics Anonymous*, 63.

Chapter 12:
Working Step Four

1. *Alcoholics Anonymous*, 3d ed. (New York: Alcoholics Anonymous World Services, Inc., 1976), 63–64.
2. *Alcoholics Anonymous*, 64.
3. *Twelve Steps and Twelve Traditions* (New York: Alcoholics Anonymous World Services, Inc., 1952), 43.
4. *Alcoholics Anonymous*, 64.
5. *Alcoholics Anonymous*, 64.
6. *Alcoholics Anonymous*, 65.
7. *Twelve Steps and Twelve Traditions*, 89.

8. The Big Book lists resentments, fears, and sexual conduct. The Twelve and Twelve lists the Seven Deadly Sins and assets.
9. *Alcoholics Anonymous,* 64.
10. *Alcoholics Anonymous,* 66.
11. *Alcoholics Anonymous,* 65.
12. The fourth column in this table is often overlooked because only three columns are shown in the example on page 65 of the AA Big Book. The fourth column of this table is clearly referred to in the third paragraph on page 67 of the AA Big Book, "When we saw our faults we listed them. We placed them before us in black and white."
13. *Alcoholics Anonymous,* 67.
14. *Alcoholics Anonymous,* 68.
15. *Alcoholics Anonymous,* 69.
16. *Twelve Steps and Twelve Traditions,* 48.
17. *Twelve Steps and Twelve Traditions,* 46.
18. *Alcoholics Anonymous,* 70.
19. *Alcoholics Anonymous,* 73.
20. *Alcoholics Anonymous,* 70.
21. *Alcoholics Anonymous,* 65.
22. The date comes from *'Pass It On,' The Story of Bill Wilson and How the A.A. Message Reached the World* (New York: Alcoholics Anonymous World Services, Inc., 1984), 127, and Thomsen, Robert, *Bill W.* (New York: Perennial Library, a division of Harper & Row Publishers, 1975), 191.
23. *'Pass It On,'* 242.
24. *Alcoholics Anonymous,* 74–75.

Chapter 13:
Working Step Five

1. *Twelve Steps and Twelve Traditions* (New York: Alcoholics Anonymous World Services, Inc., 1952), 55.
2. *Twelve Steps and Twelve Traditions,* 55.
3. *Twelve Steps and Twelve Traditions,* 58.
4. *Twelve Steps and Twelve Traditions,* 56.
5. *Twelve Steps and Twelve Traditions,* 61.
6. *Twelve Steps and Twelve Traditions,* 61.
7. *Alcoholics Anonymous,* 3d ed. (New York: Alcoholics Anonymous World Services, In., 1976), 74–75.
8. *Twelve Steps and Twelve Traditions,* 58.
9. *Twelve Steps and Twelve Traditions,* 57.

10. *Alcoholics Anonymous*, 75.
11. *Alcoholics Anonymous*, 75.
12. *Twelve Steps and Twelve Traditions*, 46.

Chapter 14:
Working Step Six

1. *Alcoholics Anonymous*, 3d ed. (New York: Alcoholics Anonymous World Services, Inc., 1976), 75–76.
2. *Twelve Steps and Twelve Traditions* (New York: Alcoholics Anonymous World Services, Inc., 1952), 63.
3. *Alcoholics Anonymous*, 76.
4. *Twelve Steps and Twelve Traditions*, 67.
5. *Twelve Steps and Twelve Traditions*, 69.
6. *Twelve Steps and Twelve Traditions*, 73.
7. *Twelve Steps and Twelve Tradition*, 65–66.
8. *Twelve Steps and Twelve Traditions*, 68.
9. *Twelve Steps and Twelve Traditions*, 68.

Chapter 15:
Working Step Seven

1. *Twelve Steps and Twelve Traditions* (New York: Alcoholics Anonymous World Services, Inc., 1952), 76.
2. *Twelve Steps and Twelve Traditions*, 70.
3. *Twelve Steps and Twelve Traditions*, 72.
4. *Twelve Steps and Twelve Traditions*, 74.
5. *Twelve Steps and Twelve Traditions*, 72.
6. *Twelve Steps and Twelve Traditions*, 75.
7. *Twelve Steps and Twelve Traditions*, 73.
8. *Alcoholics Anonymous*, 3d ed. (New York: Alcoholics Anonymous World Services, Inc., 1976), 76.

Chapter 16:
Working Step Eight

1. *Alcoholics Anonymous*, 3d ed. (New York: Alcoholics Anonymous World Services, Inc., 1976), 76.
2. *Twelve Steps and Twelve Traditions* (New York: Alcoholics Anonymous World Services, Inc., 1952), 82.
3. *Twelve Steps and Twelve Traditions*, 77.
4. *Twelve Steps and Twelve Traditions*, 81.
5. *Twelve Steps and Twelve Traditions*, 80.

6. *Twelve Steps and Twelve Traditions,* 80–81.
7. *Twelve Steps and Twelve Traditions,* 80.
8. *Twelve Steps and Twelve Traditions,* 78.
9. *Twelve Steps and Twelve Traditions,* 82.

Chapter 17:
Working Step Nine

1. *Alcoholics Anonymous,* 3d ed. (New York: Alcoholics Anonymous World Services, Inc., 1976), 76.
2. *Twelve Steps and Twelve Traditions* (New York: Alcoholics Anonymous World Services, Inc., 1952), 83.
3. *Alcoholics Anonymous,* 76.
4. *Alcoholics Anonymous,* 79.
5. *Twelve Steps and Twelve Traditions,* 85.
6. *Twelve Steps and Twelve Traditions,* 84.
7. *Twelve Steps and Twelve Traditions,* 87.
8. *Alcoholics Anonymous,* 83.
9. *Twelve Steps and Twelve Traditions,* 83.
10. *Alcoholics Anonymous,* 77–78.
11. *Alcoholics Anonymous,* 76.
12. *Alcoholics Anonymous,* 76.
13. *Twelve Steps and Twelve Traditions,* 84.

Chapter 18:
Working Step Ten

1. *Alcoholics Anonymous,* 3d ed. (New York: Alcoholics Anonymous World Services, Inc., 1976), 84–85.
2. *Alcoholics Anonymous,* 84.
3. *Twelve Steps and Twelve Traditions* (New York: Alcoholics Anonymous World Services, Inc., 1952), 89.
4. *Alcoholics Anonymous,* 84.
5. *Twelve Steps and Twelve Traditions,* 91.
6. *Alcoholics Anonymous,* 84.
7. *Twelve Steps and Twelve Traditions,* 89.
8. *Twelve Steps and Twelve Traditions,* 88.
9. *Twelve Steps and Twelve Traditions,* 93.
10. *Twelve Steps and Twelve Traditions,* 90.
11. *Twelve Steps and Twelve Traditions,* 90.
12. *Twelve Steps and Twelve Traditions,* 90.
13. *Alcoholics Anonymous,* 85.

14. *Alcoholics Anonymous,* 85.
15. *Alcoholics Anonymous,* 85.

Chapter 19:
Working Step Eleven

1. *Twelve Steps and Twelve Traditions* (New York: Alcoholics Anonymous World Services, Inc., 1952), 96.
2. *Twelve Steps and Twelve Traditions,* 98.
3. *Twelve Steps and Twelve Traditions,* 104.
4. *Twelve Steps and Twelve Traditions,* 98.
5. *As Bill Sees It: The A.A. Way of Life—Selected Writings of A.A.'s Co-Founder* (New York: Alcoholics Anonymous World Services, Inc., 1980), 264.
6. *As Bill Sees It,* 264.
7. *Alcoholics Anonymous,* 3d ed. (New York: Alcoholics Anonymous World Services, Inc., 1976), 86.
8. *Alcoholics Anonymous,* 86–87.
9. *Alcoholics Anonymous,* 87.
10. *Dr. Bob and the Good Oldtimers: A Biography, with Recollections of Early A.A. in the Midwest* (New York: Alcoholics Anonymous World Services, Inc., 1980), 314.
11. *Dr. Bob and the Good Oldtimers,* 178.
12. *Alcoholics Anonymous,* 87–88.
13. *Twelve Steps and Twelve Traditions,* 101–2.
14. *Alcoholics Anonymous,* 86.
15. *Alcoholics Anonymous,* 86.
16. *Alcoholics Anonymous Comes of Age: A Brief History of A.A.* (New York: Alcoholics Anonymous World Services, Inc., 1957), 265.
17. *Twelve Steps and Twelve Traditions,* 102.
18. *Alcoholics Anonymous,* 86.

Chapter 20:
Working Step Twelve

1. *Alcoholics Anonymous,* 3d ed. (New York: Alcoholics Anonymous World Services, Inc., 1976), 88.
2. *Twelve Steps and Twelve Traditions* (New York: Alcoholics Anonymous World Services, Inc., 1952), 106.
3. *Twelve Steps and Twelve Traditions,* 109.
4. *Twelve Steps and Twelve Traditions,* 106–7.
5. *Alcoholics Anonymous,* 569

6. *Alcoholics Anonymous,* 570
7. *Alcoholics Anonymous,* 89
8. *Alcoholics Anonymous Comes of Age: A Brief History of A.A.* (New York: Alcoholics Anonymous World Services, Inc., 1957), 71.
9. *Alcoholics Anonymous Comes of Age,* 71.
10. *Alcoholics Anonymous Comes of Age,* 139–40.
11. *Twelve Steps and Twelve Traditions,* 111–12.
12. *Twelve Steps and Twelve Traditions,* 123.
13. *Twelve Steps and Twelve Traditions,* 124.

Chapter 21:
Progress, Not Perfection

1. *Dr. Bob and the Good Oldtimers: A Biography, with Recollections of Early A.A. in the Midwest* (New York: Alcoholics Anonymous World Services, Inc., 1980), 77.

Appendices

1. Kurtz, Ernest, *Not-God: A History of Alcoholics Anonymous,* rev. and enl. ed. (Center City, Minn.: Hazelden Educational Materials, 1991), 254.
2. *Alcoholics Anonymous Comes of Age: A Brief History of A.A.* (New York: Alcoholics Anonymous World Services, Inc., 1957), 204.
3. *Alcoholics Anonymous Comes of Age,* 204.
4. *Alcoholics Anonymous Comes of Age,* 288.

Index

A

Addiction, dual
in sponsees, 38, 47–48, 82–83
in sponsors, 48
Adultery, making amends for,
190, 194
Advice and suggestions
guidelines for giving, 16–17,
75–76, 82
list of best suggestions to give
sponsees, 61
on non-program matters, 82
what to do if sponsee doesn't
respond to, 75–76
Al-Anon, Twelve Steps for, 230
Alcoholics Anonymous (Big Book)
as authority on Twelve Steps,
88–89, 95
importance of reading, 13
writing of, 88–89, 238n8
Alcoholics Anonymous, Twelve
Steps of, 229
Amends
appropriateness of making,
177–78, 189–90, 194–95
direct versus indirect, 188–90,
194
listing of, 175–78, 180–82 (*see
also* Step Eight)
making of
harm to others as
consideration in, 177–78,
190, 194–95
in Step Nine, 177–78, 181,
188–91, 193–95, 201 (*see also*
Step Nine)
in Step Ten, 201
nature of, 187–88
Step Five and, 148
willingness to make, 177–78,
180, 191, 193 (*see also* Step
Eight)
Anonymity. *See* Confidentiality
Assets, listing for Step Four, 137,
154
Assignments, 69, 95. *See also* study
suggestions *under specific Steps*
Attendance, at Twelve Step
meetings. *See* Meetings, Twelve
Step
Automobiles, loaning of, 81–82
Availability, of sponsor, 25, 40, 43,
57

B

Behavior patterns, Step Five work
on, 147, 154. *See also* Step Five
Big Book. *See Alcoholics
Anonymous* (Big Book)

HAZELDEN INFORMATION AND EDUCATIONAL SERVICES is a division of the Hazelden Foundation, a not-for-profit organization. Since 1949, Hazelden has been a leader in promoting the dignity and treatment of people afflicted with the disease of chemical dependency.

The mission of the foundation is to improve the quality of life for individuals, families, and communities by providing a national continuum of information, education, and recovery services that are widely accessible; to advance the field through research and training; and to improve our quality and effectiveness through continuous improvement and innovation.

Stemming from that, the mission of this division is to provide quality information and support to people wherever they may be in their personal journey—from education and early intervention, through treatment and recovery, to personal and spiritual growth.

Although our treatment programs do not necessarily use everything Hazelden publishes, our bibliotherapeutic materials support our mission and the Twelve Step philosophy upon which it is based. We encourage your comments and feedback.

The headquarters of the Hazelden Foundation are in Center City, Minnesota. Additional treatment facilities are located in Chicago, Illinois; New York, New York; Plymouth, Minnesota; St. Paul, Minnesota; and West Palm Beach, Florida. At these sites, we provide a continuum of care for men and women of all ages. Our Plymouth facility is designed specifically for youth and families.

For more information on Hazelden, please call **1-800-257-7800**. Or you may access our World Wide Web site on the Internet at **http://www.hazelden.org**.